John,

Thank you for your
insight, participation & enthusiasm.
I hope it has a few nuggets
you do you own thesis for

Enjoy!

Jeff Gombi
12/6/18

Peter—
Thank you so much for
your insights and help
in making the Healthcare
Shift. Best,
Jeff

Praise for *Making the Healthcare Shift*

"Consumer and employee centricity have been hallmarks for how Novant Health has thrived for years. The advice that Jeff and Scott provide in this book will help any healthcare executive trying to ignite a cultural transformation succeed at putting the patient in the center of all they do."

Carl Armato, President and Chief
Executive Officer, Novant Health

"Many healthcare organizations claim to be patient focused. The problem is that elusive goal is ever changing, and fast! Consumers are paying more for their care, they are increasingly well informed about options, and they have experiences from other industries like Amazon which set a new bar for service and convenience. Scott Davis and Jeff Gourdji provide a clear and practical roadmap to better understand these new, empowered consumers. They provide practical lessons to transform the way healthcare providers can create high engagement experiences that mirror those patients receive every day from other industries. This book is must reading for healthcare leaders and their teams, laying out a compelling case for change and the steps required to create true consumer-centricity."

Dennis Murphy, President and Chief
Executive Officer, Indiana University Health

"This book by Scott and Jeff provides a full 360 on understanding the absolute critical drivers shaping consumer driven healthcare and on the ways healthcare companies are racing forward to meet these tectonic shifts."

Prakash Patel, M.D., Chief Operating Officer, GuideWell & Florida Blue President, GuideWell Health
(note: Dr. Patel joined Anthem as Executive Vice President and President, Diversified Business Group in August 2018)

"At Cigna, we've learned that customers engage most when we can personalize the experience and meet them where they are, seamlessly, across their modality of choice, and in the moments that matter most to them. Scott and Jeff illustrate how our healthcare system – and consumerism in general – has evolved and companies must adapt and challenge themselves to lead the way."

Lisa Bacus, EVP, Global Chief Marketing & Customer Officer, Cigna

"At Geisinger Health, we learned that a fundamental change in the patient's experience requires a bolt stance to service commitment. We implemented ProvenExperience, a 'satisfaction guaranteed,' approach that many other non-healthcare service industries have embraced decades ago. Scott and Jeff illustrate through their comprehensive analysis how the healthcare industry is making the shift to a consumer-centric transformation. They provide examples of systems that are motivated to experiment, rapidly prototype, personalize and coordinate care across the entire patient journey."

Alistair Erskine M.D., Chief Informatics Officer, Geisinger Health System (note: Dr. Erskine joined Partners Healthcare as Chief Digital Health Officer in July 2018)

"Patient as consumer – a natural thought to business persons, not so natural for medical institutions, physicians and other care providers. The bond between patient and those that provide care is as old as the Hippocratic Oath. But patient needs have changed and those charged with their care need to adapt. Scott Davis and Jeff Gourdji have provided a road-map for care institutions which addresses the needs of today's patient-consumer. Their advice is practical, actionable, and rooted with rich examples. It is worth a careful read."

Bernie Ferrari, M.D., Professor and Dean,
The Johns Hopkins Carey Business School

"I learned from my own personal experience how fragmented and frustrating today's healthcare system can be when dealing with a chronic condition. Scott and Jeff capture both the challenge and the opportunity for digital health startups like One Drop to either disrupt or partner with healthcare organizations to catalyze a transformation."

Jeff Dachis, CEO, One Drop

"Many healthcare leaders overlook the criticality of the role of consumer in both differentiating and driving success. Davis and Gourdji give a clear roadmap for not only introducing consumerism into healthcare, globally, but to creating lasting change across the entire business of health."

Philip Kotler, S.C. Johnson & Son Distinguished Professor of
International Marketing, Kellogg School of Management,
Northwestern University

"Great insights on the challenges and trends in healthcare today – and the shifts taking place to better address the needs of consumers."

Christian Wards, Director of Group Healthcare, AIA Group

"Consumerists, as defined in *Making the Healthcare Shift*, have potential to be critical enablers of the transformation of healthcare. Scott & Jeff show practical examples of how leader focus on the consumer brings meaningful change to healthcare organizations."

Brooke Clarke, Global Head of Group Corporate Affairs, Hikma Pharmaceuticals

"*Making the Healthcare Shift* is an important book for leaders in healthcare. It highlights the five key shifts required to become truly consumer-centric. It is all too easy to be process or technology focused. The more promising approach is to build healthcare solutions around the patient."

Tim Calkins, Clinical Professor of Marketing, Kellogg School of Management, Northwestern University

Making the Healthcare Shift

Making the
Healthcare
Shift: The Transformation to Consumer - Centricity

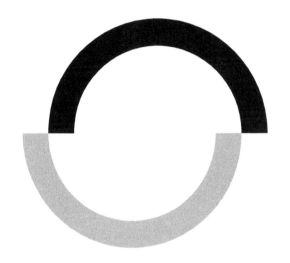

SCOTT M. DAVIS
JEFF GOURDJI

NEW YORK

LONDON • NASHVILLE • MELBOURNE • VANCOUVER

Making the Healthcare Shift
The Transformation to Consumer-Centricity

Published in New York, New York, by Morgan James Publishing. Morgan James is a trademark of Morgan James, LLC. www.MorganJamesPublishing.com

ISBN 9781642791013 paperback
ISBN 9781642791105 case laminate
ISBN 9781642791020 eBook
Library of Congress Control Number: 2018944920

Cover Design by:
Michelle Kwan,
Senior Designer, Prophet

Interior Design by:
Chris Treccani
www.3dogcreative.net

Morgan James is a proud partner of Habitat for Humanity Peninsula and Greater Williamsburg. Partners in building since 2006.

Get involved today! Visit
MorganJamesPublishing.com/giving-back

Table of Contents

Acknowledgements

Making the Healthcare Shift is the product of combined efforts, thoughts, and creativity of people who we have had the honor of working with over the years and people who we have just begun to building relationships with. First and foremost, we must thank all the healthcare experts from across the industry and the globe that gave us their valuable time to speak with us about their experiences in the industry and share what they are doing to make healthcare better for patients. Their thoughtful contributions helped us shape the premise of this book and guided our thinking. Their work and passion in this industry is inspiring and gives us hope for a stronger healthcare experience in the future. Their names are listed at the end of this section.

We owe an enormous thank you to Jessica Donald and Claire Bennett. From the conception of this project through the completion of this book, Jess and Claire have been invaluable thought partners and contributors. They have challenged us to think differently, and made this a far better product than it would have been without them. We are grateful for their enthusiasm and passion throughout.

We also are thankful for many other thought partners throughout the development of the book. First to Paul Schrimpf and Ed Rhoads who are colleagues inside Prophet's healthcare practice, and invaluable sounding boards throughout the completion of this book.

Thank you to Jeff Docherty and Jeff Hennige for developing our consumer centricity culture playbook report, which became a key chapter of *Making the Healthcare Shift*. Their hard work and thinking helped us better understand one of the most important elements that runs throughout this book. To Nicolle D'Onofrio and Tom Han for their contributions and expertise in digital transformation and what it means for healthcare. Their curiosity in and exploration of this topic, helped develop an understanding of another key theme that runs throughout this book. To Christine Brandt Jones and Joanne McDonough for their thought partnership on how to amplify and optimize consumer insights at organizations. To Helen Rosethorn whose work in culture building helped us better understand how to build a consumer-centric culture at healthcare organizations. To Fred Geyer, Sian Davies, Jay Milliken, and Julie Purser for their thought partnership on how our admittedly US-centric orientation was applicable to European and Asian markets and helping us make the shifts described in this book relevant around the globe. And to Susan Etlinger, whose expertise in artificial intelligence helped us understand the possibilities for healthcare.

Furthermore, we could not have done this work without the support of many colleagues and friends who connected us with the healthcare experts featured in this book. These include Michael Dunn, Kevin O'Donnell, Jonathan Chajet, Maria Gil, Sam Walter, Jill Steele, Jacqueline Thng, Andy Pierce, Dari Yerushalmi, and Adam Proops. Thank you for helping us rekindle old relationships and build new ones.

Thank you to a great support team at Prophet who helped present our work and share it with the world. We are grateful to Carter Holt, Eliza Robson, Mikaela Mattes, Lindsay Malone, Kelly Redling, Katie Lamkin, Amanda Nizzere, Julia Dennison, Amy Bennett, Jamie Jaturasil, Hayley Grunebaum, Jane Schumacher and John Baglivo.

Thank you to Michelle Kwan, Andres Nicholls and the Prophet design team for their work on the cover of this book.

We would be remiss if we did not express deep gratitude for the people behind the scenes. A big thank you to Kirsten Cimmarusti and Tracy Riordan for their hard work and patience juggling multiple, everchanging calendars to make our conversations with experts possible. Thank you to Sarah Mahoney and Jane Zarem for their editing and proofing support.

Additional thank you's to David Aaker and Charlene Li for their support and inspiration throughout the writing and publication process. Their knowledge and guidance was invaluable throughout this entire process and pushed us to write the best book we could.

A special thank you to the team at Morgan James Publishing for their support and production of this book.

Finally, to our families, whose patience and love during our time away while writing kept us going. Thank you to Debbie, Benjamin, Ethan and Emma Davis, and thank you to Susan Gradman and Benji, Josh and Evan Gourdji. You inspire us and bring us joy more than you know.

-Scott M Davis & Jeff Gourdji, July 2018

Our experts...
- Alistair Erskine, M.D., Chief Informatics Officer, Geisinger Health System *(joined Partners Healthcare in July 2018)*
- Andrew Dreyfus, Chief Executive Officer, Blue Cross Blue Shield of Massachusetts
- Angela Hwang, Group President, Pfizer Essential Health
- Bill Valle, CEO North America, Fresenius Medical Care
- Brad Gescheider, Senior Director Care Solutions, PatientsLikeMe

- Brent Stutz, Senior Vice President, Commercial Technologies CTO, Cardinal Health
- Carl Armato, Chief Executive Officer, Novant Health
- Chris Fanning, Chief Marketing Officer, Geisinger Health Plan
- Christian Wards, Director of Healthcare, AIA
- Craig Kartchner, former Senior Director Marketing, Intermountain Healthcare *(joined Honor Health in 2017)*
- Dan Liljenquist, Vice President, Enterprise Initiative Office, Intermountain Healthcare
- Dan Unger, Senior Vice President, Product Development, Health Catalyst
- Dave Dennis, Senior Director, Strategy and Business Development, Cardinal Health
- David Edelman, Chief Marketing Officer, Aetna
- Dave Marek, Vice President, General Manager Neuroscience, Amgen
- Dave Moore, former Senior Director Global Insights and Analytics, Eli Lilly & Company
- David Duvall, Senior Vice President, Chief Marketing & Communications, Novant Health
- David Polston, Vice President, Corporate Marketing, Anthem
- Dennis Murphy, Chief Executive Officer, Indiana University Health
- Doug Cottings, Staff Vice President, Market Strategy & Insights, Anthem
- John H. Noseworthy, M.D., President & Chief Executive Officer, Mayo Clinic
- Dusty Majumdar, PhD, former Chief Marketing Officer, Watson Health

- Eddie Segel, Senior Vice President of Business, Oscar Health
- Frank Cunningham, Vice President Managed Care, Eli Lilly & Company
- George Sauter, Chief Strategy Officer, John Muir Health
- Jean-Michel Cossery, former Vice President of Oncology North America, Eli Lilly & Company
- Jeff Dachis, Chief Executive Officer, One Drop
- Jeff Staples, Chief Operating Officer, United Family Healthcare
- Jeff Yuan, General Manager, Health Systems, Zocdoc
- Jeremy Young, Chief Marketing Officer, Sun Life Financial
- Jessica Nora, Executive Director Patient Engagement Strategy, Amgen
- Jill Chandor, Division Chair of Brand Strategy and Creative Studio, Mayo Clinic
- John Haney, Area Vice President Southeast, Johnson & Johnson
- Julia Morton, Senior Director Customer Success, Flatiron
- Kailas Nair, Vice President, Strategy and Partnerships, Vitality
- Katie Logan, Vice President, Experience, Piedmont Healthcare
- Keith Karem, Vice President of Global Marketing, Vitality
- Kelly Jo Golson, Senior Vice President, Chief Marketing & Digital Officer, Advocate Aurora Health
- Kevin Brown, Chief Executive Officer, Piedmont Healthcare
- Kevin Kumler, President, Hospital and Health System Business, Zocdoc
- Laura McKeaveney, Global Head of Patient Advocacy, Novartis
- Lee Shapiro, Managing Partner, 7wire Ventures

- Lisa Bacus, EVP, Global Chief Marketing & Customer Officer, Cigna
- Lou Zollo, former Director of Global Portfolio Development, Teva
- Lucas Pauls, Plan Sponsor Channel Lead, Mount Sinai Health System
- Marc Harrison, M.D., Chief Executive Officer, Intermountain Healthcare
- Margaret Coughlin, former Chief Marketing Officer, Mount Sinai Health System
- Mark Modesto, Chief Marketing Executive, Northwestern Medicine
- Matt Gove, Chief Consumer Officer, Piedmont Healthcare
- Matthias Krebs, Senior Director, Insights & Analytics, Novant Health
- Michael Evers, former Executive Vice President Technology, Marketing, and Operations, PatientsLikeMe
- Mike Yost, Vice President Marketing, Outreach and Experience, Indiana University Health
- Monique Levy, Executive Vice President of Business Partnerships and Solutions, PatientsLikeMe
- Natalie Schneider, Vice President Digital Health, Samsung Electronics America
- Niyum Gandhi, Executive Vice President Population Health, Mount Sinai Health System
- Patrick Blair, Chief Marketing and Consumer Officer, Anthem
- Paul Fonteyne, Chief Executive Officer, Boehringer Ingelheim USA
- Peter Corfield, Chief Commercial Officer, Spire Healthcare

- Prakash Patel, M.D., COO Guidewell & Florida Blue and President GuideWell Health, Guidewell & Florida Blue *(joined Anthem in August 2018)*
- Rey Martinez, former Senior Vice President, Chief Marketing and Communications Officer, Presence Health
- Rob Odom, Vice President of Marketing and Brand Management, UCSF Medical Center
- Robin Glasco, Chief Innovation Officer, Blue Cross Blue Shield of Massachusetts
- Sean Burke, Chief Executive Officer Asia Pacific, GE HealthCare
- Serge Raffard, Asia Head of Strategy, Product, Health, MetLife
- Sheri Dodd, Vice President and General Manager, Medtronic Care Management Services
- Stacey Geffken, Director, Product Development and Market Research, Geisinger Health Plan
- Stephanie Lim, Head of Marketing, Alpine Cluster Alcon, A Novartis Division
- Stephanie Papes, founder & Chief Executive Officer, Boulder Care
- Sterling Lanier, Chief Executive Officer, Tonic Health
- Susan Ringdal, Vice President Corporate Strategy & Investor Relations, Hikma Pharmaceuticals
- Thane Wettig, Chief Marketing Officer and Metabolic Franchise Head, Intarcia Therapeutics, Inc.
- Tom Feitel, Global Head, Enterprise Customer Solutions, Medocity
- Veronica Chase, Vice President, Marketing, Eli Lilly & Company

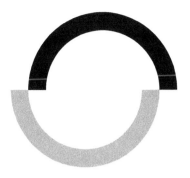

Preface

The Case for Consumer Centricity in Healthcare

THE ERA OF THE E-CONSUMER

Change has been on the horizon for many years for healthcare organizations, both in how they do business and in how they engage consumers. In the past, experts discussed the need for healthcare organizations to drive preference and selection–how organizations convince consumers that they are the best hospital, best plan or most-effective medication. But the healthcare landscape has changed drastically from when these discussions first began; conversations have shifted focus to driving engagement, relationships and loyalty— much like other consumer businesses. Today's healthcare world belongs to the "e-consumer."

The e-consumer, despite the name, is not a technology term. The genesis is the "e-patient," a concept coined in the 1990s by the late Tom Ferguson, M.D., an American physician who advocated for participatory medicine and the increasing role of the patient in managing their own healthcare. E-patients, he says, are **empowered, engaged, equipped and enabled**. As the internet united patients with information and communication, a shift was needed in the balance of power in healthcare. Patients needed to be treated as powerful participants in their own health in partnership with physicians. E-patients are not just patients who engage for purposes of self-diagnosis. These individuals also engage in their own health management, partnering closely with organizations in order to find the solutions that work best for them. It is a partnership grounded in both the patient's need and the expertise of the physician.

The e-patient, however, is a concept limited to direct interactions with healthcare organizations. While those interactions are key parts of the healthcare journey, the majority of an individual's life takes place outside healthcare organizations. It is important that patients are engaged when they are ill; but their behavior outside the clinic, hospital or doctor's office has significant implications and cannot be disregarded. That's why we have expanded the concept of the e-patient and evolved it into the e-consumer. Similar to the e-patient, the e-consumer is **empowered, engaged, equipped and enabled**; however, the e-consumer does not only exist when interacting with the healthcare system, as traditionally defined, when things have gone wrong or someone is sick. For the e-consumer, moments of health are just as important as moments of sickness. Serving e-consumers means considering them at all stages of life, especially when they are not in the clinic. Serving e-consumers means giving them tools to track their health, providing them with education that sees them through recovery and beyond and designing services that cure and empower them.

In the e-consumer era, healthcare organizations must develop products, services and experiences that align with consumer needs. The only way to do that is to become consumer-centric. The understanding that healthcare organizations have of consumers should mirror the understanding that companies like Amazon, Zappos and Netflix have of their consumers. Operations and services need to revolve around the consumer, not the other way around. Whether a provider, payer or life science company, consumer centricity in healthcare requires that every team, service line and department exist to serve the consumer in a remarkable way at every stage of the healthcare journey. For healthcare organizations, that means engaging consumers in the healthcare system and enabling them to become proactive participants in their own health. Consumer centricity opens the door to greater possibilities of proactive health management and greater opportunities for bringing healthcare to consumers around the world, benefiting both individual organizations and society as a whole.

THE GROWING POPULATION OF E-CONSUMERS

Healthcare organizations have existed for many years in the world of the e-consumer, but only recently have they have begun taking steps to adapt to consumers' needs. In the past, e-consumers were only those individuals set on being proactive managers of their own health. They were frustrated by the fragmented nature of their experiences. They wanted healthcare to be like Apple, offering experiences that are accessible, intuitive, connected and seamless. Today, the rising costs of healthcare are making it imperative for consumers to be engaged in their own health. Individuals who weren't e-consumers before are joining the movement and demanding more from healthcare organizations.

Around the world, individuals have an enormous investment stake in their own healthcare. In the United States, which has a primarily market-driven healthcare system in which the patient carries a heavy financial burden, the cost of medicine continues to rise rapidly. Between 2006 and 2015, out-of-pocket costs per patient nearly doubled.[1] Since the rollout of the Affordable Care Act (ACA), the number of high-deductible plans has dramatically increased. From 2016 to 2017, the number of adults with a high-deductible plan increased from 26 percent to 39 percent.[2] The deductibles themselves have increased by 67 percent.[3] Moreover, those who are covered by their employers have experienced an 83 percent increase in their individual contributions to their health plans.[4] When individuals are responsible for these debilitating costs, their choices can have significant personal and financial impact. Consumers directly control an estimated $330 billion annually in out-of-pocket healthcare expenses. The choices they make potentially affect 61 percent of all healthcare spending.[5] In a healthcare system such as this, high prices lead to changes in behavior.

In European nations, where healthcare is largely provided by the government, consumers also experience financial pressures. Between 2006 and 2016, Germans saw a 150 percent increase in the cost of their mandatory health insurance per capita.[6] Over the same period,

---

1   http://kff.org/report-section/ehbs-2015-summary-of-findings/

2   https://www.beckershospitalreview.com/payer-issues/cdc-nearly-40-of-us-adults-have-high-deductible-health-plans.html

3   Ibid

4   Ibid

5   https://healthcare.mckinsey.com/enabling-healthcare-consumerism

6   https://www.destatis.de/DE/ZahlenFakten/GesellschaftStaat/Gesundheit/Gesundheitsausgaben/Gesundheitsausgaben.html

the United Kingdom experienced a 150 percent increase in public-health expenditures, as demand for care grew and the population aged.[7] And, in Switzerland, where healthcare is also covered by the government, out-of-pocket health expenditures increased 120 percent from 2008 to 2014.[8]

In China, where the healthcare system has undergone significant change along with shifts in the government, patients are deeply dissatisfied with their coverage. Nearly 40 percent of Chinese citizens who receive public coverage report being dissatisfied.[9] The future of costs in the country looks grim, with a predicted 330 percent increase in Chinese insurance premium revenues from 2014 to 2020.[10]

These global financial pressures are the new reality. The heavy financial burden of healthcare is driving consumers to take more time considering the price, value and necessity of the care they believe they need. For consumers who shop for care, the experience is far more difficult than comparison shopping for other consumer products. In fact, certain policies make comparison shopping nearly impossible. In 2016, 43 U.S. states lacked any laws setting a minimum standard for the type of healthcare price information accessible to patients. Still, we see that in non-emergency and non-life-threatening situations, some healthcare consumers take a more strategic approach to selecting care. In 2014, about 56 percent of Americans searched

7   http://www.ukpublicspending.co.uk/spending_
     chart_1900_2020UKb_17c1li011mcn_10t

8   https://www.bfs.admin.ch/bfs/en/home/statistics/health.assetdetail.1160151.
     html

9   http://www.ey.com/Publication/vwLUAssets/EY-the-rise-of-private-health-
     insurance-in-china/$FILE/EY-the-rise-of-private-health-insurance-in-china.pdf

10   http://expatfinancial.com/growth-in-private-health-coverage-in-china-impacts-
     expats/

price information before receiving healthcare[11] and more than one-fifth compared prices from multiple providers.[12] This shopping is most evident for medications. In recent years, new services have entered the scene that simplify shopping. GoodRX, for example, is a website and app that allows consumers to compare the price of various drugs at their local pharmacies. The service not only enables price comparison but also provides the consumer with coupons and vouchers to help offset some of the costs. While there is no data on how much this research impacts final decision making, it is clear that consumers do take the research into account.

In addition to researching care options by price and quality, consumers also opt for less expensive options, such as retail and urgent care clinics that offer services for non-life-threatening illnesses like ear infections or sore throats at a price 40 to 80 percent below a visit with the doctor. Blue Cross Blue Shield Association saw the number of members who visited a retail clinic nearly double from 2012 to 2017.[13]

HEALTHCARE MUST RESPOND QUICKLY

Even as the e-consumer movement strengthened and people demanded more, healthcare organizations had little incentive to embrace consumer centricity. They lacked market competition to push them and, even though consumers were feeling financial pressure, the organizations had no real financial incentive to change. This is no longer the case. Today, beyond the rise in consumer expectations, healthcare organizations have two strong motives that are pushing

---

11   http://www.modernhealthcare.com/article/20170415/MAGAZINE/304159998

12   http://www.modernhealthcare.com/article/20170415/MAGAZINE/304159998

13   https://www.forbes.com/sites/brucejapsen/2017/01/18/retail-clinic-use-soars-but-not-for-obamacare-patients/#7bdcc14d62a8

them to change: 1) the increasing financial strain on the overall industry, and 2) emerging innovative competitors from both inside and outside the category.

FINANCIAL PROBLEMS ARE INTENSIFYING

Financially strained healthcare financers, including employers and governments around the world, have limited funding to cover the increasing costs and growing needs of an aging population. As a result, these entities are transforming reimbursement models and pushing healthcare organizations to deliver better results at lower costs. Many of these entities recognize, however, that the best approach is engagement. They understand that, when patients are involved in their own care, they spend more time outside the clinic being healthy and less time inside the clinic being sick.

The State of Healthcare in the United States

Arguably, the most striking case of financial pressure is in the United States—where the cost of care is crippling for both patients and organizations. In 2015, U.S. healthcare costs were $3.2 trillion. This translates to annual healthcare costs of $10,348 per person in 2016 versus just $146 per person in 1960. In the United States, the cost of healthcare has risen faster than annual income.[14] Possibly more concerning is that half of that spending was attributed to the sickest five percent of the population. To control the ballooning costs, the market-driven healthcare system is moving in the direction of value-based care. Legislation like the Affordable Care Act (ACA) and Medicare Access and CHIP Reauthorization Act (MACRA) set the stage for value-based care in Medicare, and private insurers began to follow suit. In 2016, McKesson commissioned a study conducted by

---

14   https://www.thebalance.com/causes-of-rising-healthcare-costs-4064878

ORC International that explored the transition from fee-for-service to value-based care. The payers surveyed predict that, by 2021, 60 percent of providers will participate in value-based arrangements and 54 percent of all reimbursements will be paid through value-based care models.[15] The move to value-based care is happening even at pharmaceutical companies. Today, 25 percent of health plans already have at least one outcomes-based contract with a drug manufacturer, and 30 percent of health plans are currently negotiating one or more such contracts.[16] In a value-based care model, change must be the new mandate for healthcare organizations. It is imperative that consumers are engaged in ways that allow them to proactively manage and, as much as possible, take accountability for their own health; their personal finances and the financial success of healthcare organizations both depend on it.

The State of Healthcare Around the Globe

Like the United States, where reimbursement models are changing in response to rising costs, publicly funded healthcare systems are being squeezed as well, causing inefficiencies and long wait times. The U.K.'s National Health Service (NHS), which enjoyed a surplus of £2 billion in 2009-10, suffered a deficit of £1 billion in 2015—a 143 percent plummet in six years.[17] And by the third quarter of 2016,

---

15　http://mhsinfo3.mckesson.com/rs/834-UAW-463/images/VBR-Study-2016v112016.pdf?mkt_tok=eyJpIjoiTldZeE9HVmtOVEF5TkRGbCIsIn-QiOiI1VlI2aFhCanFqazhzazdac0M4bndpK0ZvOTBcL1BpbWRTMHd-SWmU1RW42d0NjVHJxVG5hemhtMnVOYWVYUkY2dU5YeDc5WX-VtSFd0M2xsazd6c3BRUkJzSTdkNmxEcEh3d0ttK1ZEdFFFcL1JrZmlXalFEWm-RMM2ZkV2JVREVkMnhzIn0%3D

16　https://www.beckershospitalreview.com/payer-issues/payers-estimate-59-of-payments-will-be-value-based-by-2021-5-quick-stats.html

17　http://www.independent.co.uk/news/uk/politics/nhs-deficit-crisis-one-chart-that-shows-how-the-nhs-is-headed-for-financial-ruin-a6687926.html the NHS was operating at a deficit of £990 million pounds.[18] With the NHS in financial crisis, Parliament has been attempting to put in measures that focus more on value. In 2016, in an effort to lower costs and drive efficiency, it implemented NHS RightCare, a program meant to increase value across systems through the use of data and innovation.[19]

In China, the health system is experiencing a different kind of havoc. With only 1.5 doctors for every 1,000 patients, wait times are long, hospitals are overcrowded, doctors are overworked and patients are taking matters into their own hands to express frustration—in some instances even resorting to violence.[20] These pressures have led companies in the private sector, like Tencent and Alibaba, to make investments in companies such as the WeDoctor Group, which offers telemedicine and online prescriptions as a way to serve patients and take some of the burden off physicians.[21]

Around the world, countries are in crisis situations and are discovering that the way they engage patients today is no longer sustainable. Without change, they will face powerful economic, public health and political consequences. Partnering with consumers in a way that engages and empowers them will not just be a point of difference for healthcare organizations but a point of survival.

---

18   https://www.kingsfund.org.uk/blog/2017/03/impact-nhs-financial-pressures-mixed-picture

19   https://www.england.nhs.uk/wp-content/uploads/2017/02/board-papers-090217-item-6-nhs-rightcare.pdf

20   https://www.nytimes.com/2018/01/31/technology/amazon-china-health-care-ai.html

21   https://www.nytimes.com/2018/01/31/technology/amazon-china-health-care-ai.html

EMERGING COMPETITORS ARE A CONSTANT THREAT

In addition to evolving to meet the financial needs of healthcare financers, organizations must constantly evolve in order to avoid being displaced or marginalized by smaller, more innovative consumer-centric players like the WeDoctor Group mentioned above or Oscar Health, which we will explore later. With all the changes that have occurred in the healthcare landscape, the industry has seen the emergence of companies that assume traditional healthcare roles but execute them in a more consumer-centric way. In publicly funded systems, financial constraints are opening the door for innovative private organizations to attract consumers who can afford their services. China, for example, saw a 63 percent increase in spending on medicines, healthcare products and services between 2013 and 2014 on retail giant Alibaba's sites.[22] These more innovative companies have considerable healthcare potential and continue to gain ground, as consumers push for new ways to engage with healthcare organizations. These smaller organizations typically focus on a narrow portion of the healthcare system and do not have nearly the financial impact or market share of traditional players; however, they are playing an increasingly important role in finding new ways to approach the delivery of care. In many ways, this phenomenon is mirroring the total disruption of the retail category, where traditional stalwarts like Sears, Kmart, JCPenney, Macy's and others have been replaced by online giants such as Amazon, Alibaba and eBay—as well as by niche players such as Sephora and H&M.

Oscar Health

Take, for example, American company Oscar Health, a small digital insurer created for the individual exchanges after the passing of the ACA. Oscar offers an array of different individual health plans, helps consumers seamlessly select a plan that best fits their needs, easily connects patients with providers via its online app and offers a comprehensive concierge service to assist consumers. Oscar operates only in select regions of six states (as of 2018) and has faced financial challenges due to the instability of the individual exchanges. But the company has demonstrated, through partnering with large health systems such as The Cleveland Clinic and delivering a strong consumer experience, that health insurance does not need to be frustrating.

One Medical

Another example of a player changing the game is One Medical, a small, member-based, primary care provider that has been entering major metropolitan areas across the United States. The organization takes a different approach to delivering care, with 24/7 secured communications with patients, same-day appointments and patient evaluations that allow providers to understand their patients as whole people. This digitally native provider, while still in its infancy, has designed a new model for how consumers experience primary care.

DoctorCare Anywhere

This digital general-practitioner service is based primarily in the United Kingdom but also has select services internationally. The company's program brings health to consumers' fingertips, providing telemedicine, health-tracking programs and other concierge services.[23] While DoctorCare Anywhere is a small, private company within a

---

23   https://www.healthcarebusinessinternational.com/awards/doctor-care-anywhere-best-patient-platform-winner-2017/

public system, it opens the door to new possibilities for the NHS to leverage digital to boost engagement and drive down costs.

Parkway Pantai

Parkway Pantai is one of Asia's largest private healthcare groups, with hospitals in Singapore, Malaysia, India, China, Brunei and the United Arab Emirates. The concierge medical provider is known for best-in-class patient experiences and outcomes. While its consumers are almost exclusively wealthy Asians and immigrants, the outcomes from its premier concierge services that guide patients through the journey are showing the possibilities and benefits of holistic care.

While small and focused, these nimble players are setting the groundwork for new models of care delivery and could become greater competition. As the times change and the possibilities for care grow, these small players are not something that traditional organizations should take lightly.

TECHNOLOGY IS REWRITING THE RULES OF CHANGE

With frustrated and financially strained healthcare consumers and healthcare financers, it is clear that organizations must find a way to better engage patients and keep them healthy. In the United States, it is a matter of staying relevant and competitive as an organization; and for publicly funded services around the world, it's a matter of maintaining the economic stability of a system responsible for the care of an entire nation. While this is a huge undertaking for healthcare organizations around the globe, the rise of technology and digital innovation gives these organizations a considerable opportunity and a large platform to engage patients in new, impactful and more effective ways.

Over the years, we have seen technology revolutionize the way traditional services are delivered—whether the service is cellular, entertainment, retail or even dating. The most obvious example of this is in the transportation industry, with ride-share economy stars like Uber and Lyft. The technology of those companies has revolutionized the way people navigate cities across the globe. Even for individuals who prefer public transit, technology has changed the experience. Public transit systems now update commuters with faster and more accurate information about their travels, send out alerts in a timely manner and help commuters get where they need to be in the way they want to get there. Even in highly regulated industries like financial services, technology has changed the game. Consumers have greater access and control over their money and their relationship with banks. The ability of consumers to manage their money how and when they want has made banking far less frustrating. Technology has also fundamentally changed the way we consume entertainment with the personalized and customized services of Netflix, for example. And, it has changed the way we shop, with Amazon creating a marketplace where consumers can simultaneously compare prices and quality. The changes in these industries give us a window into what the intersection between technology and healthcare might be.

People consume healthcare services in fundamentally different ways than they do other services. But, as technology continues to make experiences seamless and customized, more consumers will begin to expect and demand the same from healthcare as they have from other industries.

This intersection between technology and healthcare makes consumer centricity possible in three key ways:

Serving as a Platform for Information Exchange

Technology has led to the democratization of healthcare information. Today, consumers have unlimited access to: medical information about various health conditions; online communities of patients who share stories and experiences; and reviews of physicians, medications and hospitals. Some of those resources contribute to the consumer's decision making. For example, 60 percent of Americans use physician review websites like HealthGrades, RateMDs and Vital when selecting a provider.[24] Other resources connect groups of patients with similar conditions. In a 2014 study, 37 percent of patients with a chronic condition reported having read someone else's commentary or experience about health or medical issues on an online news group, website or blog.[25] These resources provide consumers with relevant information that ultimately affects behavior. In fact, in the same 2014 study, more than 40 percent of consumers reported that information they find via social media affects the way they deal with their health decisions.[26] Take, for example, organizations like PatientsLikeMe, which offer a space for patients to share experiences with different treatments and conditions, facilitating connections among patients and collecting anecdotal data on their experiences with various treatments. PatientsLikeMe and services like it have opened up a whole new world of technology-infused experiences for patients who thought they were on their own. These platforms are a perfect model for healthcare organizations to leverage for connecting with, and advocating for, patients on a personal level.

Facilitating Primary Data Gathering

The rise of digital health has blurred the lines between consumer products and health products by enabling consumers to monitor

---

24 https://www.consumerreports.org/doctors/online-doctor-ratings-why-you-cant-always-rely/

25 http://www.pewinternet.org/2010/03/24/social-media-and-health/

26 https://www.cdc.gov/minorityhealth/summit/2016/promotinghealthequitythroughsocialmedia.pdf

their symptoms, manage their conditions and track their health on a consistent basis. Products such as the Apple Watch, Fitbit and other data-collecting devices such as AlivCor's, which records EKGs via smartphones, are putting our health in our pockets and on our wrists. A study conducted by Accenture in 2016 found that 78 percent of U.S. consumers wear, or would be willing to wear, technology for health tracking. Fifteen percent of those consumers would be willing to use wearable devices for fitness/lifestyle only; 12 percent, for vital signs only. More than half of the consumers polled would use wearables for both.[27] In addition to remote tracking and monitoring devices, consumers also use phone apps for health management. The number of consumers who use mobile health apps increased from 16 percent in 2014 to 33 percent in 2016.[28] These products and programs allow consumers, both healthy and unhealthy, to track and own their health data and to set personal goals for improving their health. The fact that technology can track consumers' behaviors both inside and outside the clinic makes it easier for healthcare organizations to understand the various factors that contribute to consumers' health. With this knowledge, organizations will not only be able to make advances in life-saving treatments, but also will be able to understand the best ways to influence the health of consumers outside their four walls. Having that amount of knowledge also enables organizations to leverage rich sources of data to customize and personalize experiences in a way that better engages consumers.

---

27   https://www.accenture.com/us-en/insight-research-shows-patients-united-states-want-heavy

28   https://www.accenture.com/us-en/insight-research-shows-patients-united-states-want-heavy

Granting Consumers Ownership of Their Healthcare Data

Healthcare apps and consumer health products have led to the generation of enormous amounts of healthcare data, from consumers' vital signs and nutrition intake to their daily activity levels. In addition, the advent of Electronic Health Records (EHR) and their accelerated adoption in the United States since the ACA was put into effect has led to a new world in which clinical and provider data is consolidated into a single system. Digital startups have even stepped in to make this data collection easier. Tonic Health is an online patient data-collection company that partners with providers to gather information in a gamified and engaging way. *The New England Journal of Medicine* estimates that up to 30 percent of the entire world's stored data is generated within healthcare. A single patient alone produces nearly 80 megabytes each year in imaging and EHR data. This has such clear clinical, financial and operational value for healthcare organizations that it is estimated the data could enable more than $300 billion annually in reduced costs.[29] What is perhaps even more remarkable is the amount of this data that consumers produce and own themselves. Take the Apple Watch, for example, which stores enormous amounts of data about the wearer's activity levels and heart rate. By giving consumers their own personal health-data ownership, technology opens the door to patient empowerment and accountability—which can greatly increase engagement.

MASSIVE MERGERS MAKE CHANGE URGENT

After many years of discussion about what transformation in healthcare means and what it might look like (on both the professional side and the consumer side), the world has started seeing some big announcements and proclamations. In 2017, CVS and Aetna

---

announced a partnership that would create a one-stop shop for health insurance and basic care—reimagining the way consumers receive healthcare services by leveraging and reimagining retail sites as true points of care. Following closely behind was the announcement in January 2018 by Amazon, Berkshire Hathaway and JPMorgan that they would be entering a joint venture to provide their employees with higher quality care at a lower price. Retail giant Alibaba is reinventing and digitizing the way healthcare is delivered in China's precarious system. And Walmart, the largest retailer in the world, recently announced interest in acquiring American insurer Humana. These types of partnerships will continue to be part of the ongoing healthcare dialog as companies with an interest in healthcare look for smart, efficient and lucrative ways of disrupting the market. Each has the potential to change healthcare as we know it and, most importantly, put the consumer at the center of it all.

Today, we are seeing only the beginning of consumer centricity in healthcare. Organizations are developing and delivering solutions and services in ways that are most relevant to consumers in order to drive both choice and engagement. Healthcare organizations that have previously revolved around the needs of healthcare providers are having to shift toward revolving around the needs of healthcare consumers. While there is still a long way to go to achieve full consumer centricity, traditional healthcare organizations are taking smalls steps by:

Empowering Consumers

Global pharmaceutical companies like Boehringer Ingelheim are leveraging digital health solutions to help facilitate greater and more frequent conversations between patients and their physicians.

Engaging Consumers

Payers like Aetna in the United States or AIA across Asia-Pacific are investing in engagement tools to help consumers track, monitor and manage their health on their own terms through partnerships with digital companies like Apple and Vitality.

Equipping and Enabling Consumers to Manage Their Own Health

Regional providers like Geisinger Health are building programs to tackle health problems in a way that works best for consumers. The system's FoodRX program sets up healthy food prescriptions for low-income consumers who suffer from diabetes.

As organizations work to gain their footing in the era of the e-consumer, we set out to understand how they can start to make a shift toward consumer centricity in a way that benefits them, the individual and the public at large. We believe the lessons we uncovered will go a long way in helping make this shift.

Introduction

Making the Healthcare Shift

As the healthcare industry sits on the edge of transformation, healthcare leaders recognize the need to react to changes in the industry and to begin serving the e-consumer. "In our work with healthcare providers around the world, we certainly see consumer experience rising on their list of priorities. While local demands vary due to demographics, payment and delivery models, culture or consumer expectations, the opportunity for services and technologies to address specific unmet consumer needs in healthcare is evident globally," says Sean Burke, President and CEO of Asia Pacific at GE Healthcare.

While organizations are aware that they need to transform, many do not know how to get there—let alone where to start. Transformation is an overwhelming task, and no organization has cracked the code. Many organizations interested in making the shift may have to redefine their overall purpose and values, reconsider their talent and fundamentally change the way they interact with those they serve. These organizations are at a disadvantage when it comes to consumer centricity, because they were not built to meet a basic human need nor to meet the expectations of consumers today. Providers historically have taken a paternalistic approach to care, in which the doctor always knows best. Payers were built to serve employers and to manage costs. And pharmaceutical companies have driven their business through providers, not patients. Getting to consumer centricity in healthcare is not going to be easy, given these truths. Let's explore in detail some of the barriers that stand in the way of these organizations:

A Limited View of the Health Journey

Across the healthcare spectrum, organizations have historically focused on a specific part of the health journey. Healthcare providers are structurally designed to serve patients who are sick and need treatment, not consumers who are managing their health. The focus has been on moments inside the clinic, not outside. The same has been true for pharmaceutical companies that focus only on patients at the point of choosing and administering a medication. Payers have had an even more limited view of the health journey and have only recently begun thinking of their members as the end customer. Previously, health insurers focused on the employers who signed the contracts. Healthcare organizations have long failed to consider the entire journey. "Many health systems have interpreted consumer centricity to be primarily those face-to-face moments with the doctors, nurses and other care providers," says George Sauter, Chief Strategy Officer at John Muir Health, a California-based care provider. "That is when we listen. But where we are falling down is with the systems we have in place that get patients to those moments with the care provider."

Best,

Scott Davis and Jeff Gourdji

564 W. Randolph
Suite 700
Chicago, IL 60661

T +1 312 879 1930
F +1 312 879 1940
www.prophet.com

PROPHET

Dear Expert,

Enclosed is a copy of our book *Making the Healthcare Shift: The Transformation to Consumer-Centricity*. Our conversation with you was one of over 70 conversations that, together with a quantitative study of 240 healthcare executives, formed the basis of this book. Without your participation and insight, it would not be what we believe it to be: a practical guide and playbook, rich in examples, that will help leaders make their organization more consumer-centric.

We hope you find the contents of the book valuable and relevant for your organization. With your invitation, we would be happy to present our findings to your leadership team. As you read the book, we look forward to your feedback and welcome any questions.

Those organizations cannot reach beyond the clinic and take into account the processes that bring the patients to them in the first place.

Holistic View of the Consumer Health Journey

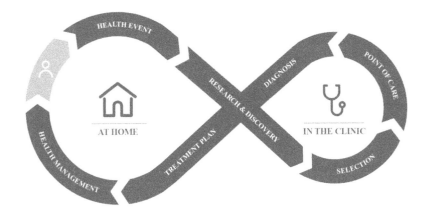

Focus on Tactical, Not Holistic, Changes

Healthcare organizations sometimes follow the steps of tech companies by latching onto trends without considering how those trends will perform in healthcare or if they are even relevant. They invest in programs like apps or updated websites, which serve only as Band-Aids for a larger problem and sometimes even make it worse. This approach leads to ineffective programs and wasteful investments. In the pharmaceutical industry alone, 26 percent of the more than 700 apps created are used only once—and nearly three-quarters of them are abandoned by the 10th use.[30]

---

30 https://www.warc.com/content/article/bestprac/using_technology_to_drive_behavioural_change_in_healthcare/120037?utm_source=DailyNews&utm_medium=email&

Hesitation to Adopt New Technology

Healthcare is a highly regulated industry in many parts of the world; so, when it comes to embracing and adopting new technologies, there is substantial hesitation and resistance. Although cloud-based technology is the wave of the future, and startups that rely on it typically get the required privacy certifications, leaders at healthcare organizations take on significant risk if they invest and something goes awry. "Change is hard—and sometimes scary—particularly when it comes to considering the technological infrastructure that enables great leaps forward, like cloud-based hosting. Attitudes are slowly shifting, but health systems and insurers are behind on implementing new technologies because they fear—rightly so—some of the security risks that come with cloud-based capabilities. But instead of considering ways to contain or protect against these risks, some folks just make it a blanket rule not to use cloud-based technologies at all," says Sterling Lanier, CEO of Tonic Health, a data collection and payments platform.

Cumbersome Legacy Systems

Adding to these challenges, many traditional healthcare organizations are not set up to succeed in making the shift to consumer centricity, because their legacy technology systems were designed for a different era. Changing, updating or making these systems more flexible requires significant structural and financial investment. The challenges here are obvious. Integrating or pulling new data into old systems is cumbersome, resulting in an inability to share and access information in a consumer-centered way. "Keeping track of and following up with patients is really challenging given cumbersome IT systems, and the burden falls on clinicians," explains Stephanie Papes, Founder and CEO of digital health startup Boulder Care. "They are overwhelmed with this administrative work, but they hesitate to take on any new technology when the technology they have is already difficult." Moreover, when it comes to collaboration with different players in the healthcare ecosystem, fragmentation is a challenge. There is no easy way for life-science companies to communicate with physicians and no easy way for providers to resolve conflicts with payers. This hinders care coordination and puts on the consumer the responsibility of connecting all the disparate pieces.

A Future of Uncertainty

On top of the structural barriers that organizations grapple with during transformation, they are also at the mercy of ever-changing healthcare policies that can uproot current structures and flip them on their head. As we have witnessed in the United States where healthcare is a highly politicized topic, in China where the form of government dictates the distribution of health and in the United Kingdom where limited funding for the National Health Service is turning into a crisis, organizations are constantly on precarious footing. "With the uncertainty in the market and the rising costs," says Mark Modesto, Chief Marketing Officer of Chicago's Northwestern Medicine, "we have to be thoughtful of how we move, because there is this general fear that all of the sudden these changes could be obsolete." In an environment of such uncertainty, the investments that true transformation require can seem not only overwhelming, but also unwise.

TRANSFORMATION TAKES TIME

Some healthcare organizations are making big moves to consumer centricity. Others are taking smaller, incremental steps. Still others are waiting on the sidelines. Regardless of where organizations are today, the transformation to consumer centricity takes significant time and change at both the system-wide and cultural levels. We find that organizations typically go through four phases of transformation:

Learning, Committing, Accelerating and Embedding. In the Learning phase, organizations understand that consumer centricity is critical but have yet to develop a definition of what transformation involves at both a strategic or a cultural level or the roadmap to get there. In the Committing phase, organizations are aligned on the key components of making the switch and have begun to identify the investments required to be more consumer-centric; however, they have not begun to make those investments in culture and processes—at least in a meaningful way. In the Accelerating phase, organizations have begun to transform through visible quick wins and internal momentum; consumer centricity is starting to be woven into the culture. In the phase we call Embedding, consumer centricity is self-sustaining, with an established culture of consumer obsession; a new way of doing business is clearly realized. In our survey of healthcare leaders, 50 percent report being in the Learning and Committing stages, with only seven percent in the Embedding stage. Many organizations have a long road ahead of them to get to consumer centricity, but our research shows that organizations are aware that change is necessary. It's a question of how to make it happen. As healthcare organizations progress through these phases, we wanted to discover which organizations were making the most progress and how their stories could help others do the same.

Four Stages of Consumer-Centric Transformation

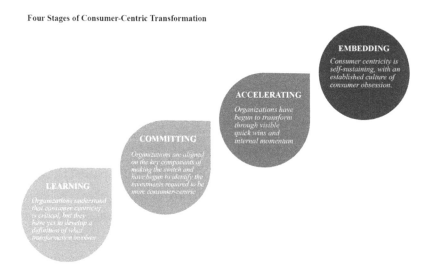

WHAT THIS RESEARCH TELLS US

To understand what the healthcare industry is currently doing and can to do to reshape itself, we conducted in-depth interviews with more than 60 organizations around the globe and surveyed almost 250 executives at leading healthcare enterprises, including large hospital systems; payers; and pharmaceutical, medical device and digital health companies in the United States, Asia and Europe. These organizations include some of the most prominent names in healthcare, including Mayo Clinic, AIA, Aetna and Pfizer. During our conversations, we set out to understand what these organizations are currently doing to be consumer-centric, where they would like to be in the future, and what challenges they face in getting to their ideal state. From our interviews, we identified five key shifts that organizations can make now to become more consumer-centric tomorrow. The shifts we identified are universal to transformation. They span the healthcare ecosystem and apply to geographies and organizations around the world. While we identified the necessity of these shifts, we also identified a growing problem. Organizations aren't making them. Our research indicates that less than 15 percent have made full progression on any of the shifts outlined, which speaks to massive opportunities from both a business and a consumer perspective. So, while pockets of organizations are catching on, there is much work to be done.

THE SHIFTS TO CONSUMER CENTRICITY IN HEALTHCARE

The shifts below cover the strategic, tactical and cultural changes that need to happen for consumer centricity to come to life. We begin with the First Shift, tackling strategic changes that set the stage for the following shifts; we end in the Fifth Shift, which addresses the internal capabilities and structures that lay the groundwork for the others and enable a consumer-obsessed culture. These shifts are not sequential and can be tackled in different ways, depending on the needs of the organization and the role of those leading the charge. We will explore these different paths in greater detail in our final chapters; but for now, let's look at each:

THE FIRST SHIFT: From Tactical Fixes to a Holistic Experience Strategy

Healthcare organizations often start enhancing consumer experiences in one-off initiatives (e.g., reducing waiting-room times). By executing on a holistic experience that ladders up to a unifying strategy, however, the organization can move to the next level of consumer centricity.

THE SECOND SHIFT: From Fragmented Care to Connected Ecosystems

Although payers, providers and pharma companies are finding new ways to work together, the healthcare journey remains fragmented for most consumers, causing frustration and inefficiency.

But when healthcare organizations operate in a connected, integrated ecosystem rather than as a stand-alone entity, they can better engage consumers and resolve the pain points that are preventing long-term health.

THE THIRD SHIFT: From Population-Centric to Person-Centered

Healthcare organizations often focus on creating products, services and experiences for groups of similar consumers, such as those who have the same condition or those who fall into the same demographic. To be truly consumer-centric, it is critical for healthcare organizations to create products, services and experiences for consumers based on their individual needs.

THE FOURTH SHIFT: From Incremental Improvements to Pervasive Innovation

Healthcare organizations often settle for small, time-consuming improvements to established systems and processes that were never designed with the consumer in mind. To put the consumer at the center, organizations must reimagine their approach to innovation in order to truly reinvent the consumer experience. Organizations can consistently adopt both an innovative and a minimally viable product mindset, using a portfolio of approaches to spark wholesale, enterprise-wide change.

THE FIFTH SHIFT: From Insights as a Department to a Culture of Consumer Obsession

Establishing insights as a function is critical to gathering intelligence, but it's not enough. Healthcare organizations can go further by creating a culture of consumer obsession, where everyone in the organization always keeps the consumer front and center.

Five Shifts Summary

THE FIRST SHIFT

From Tactical Fixes to a
Holistic Experience Strategy

Healthcare organizations often start enhancing consumer experiences in one-off initiatives (i.e., reducing waiting-room times). However, by executing on a holistic experience that ladders up to a unifying strategy, they can move their organization to the next level of consumer centricity.

THE SECOND SHIFT

From Fragmented Care to
Connected Ecosystems

Although payers, providers and pharma companies are finding new ways to work together, the healthcare journey remains fragmented for most consumers, causing frustration and inefficiency. But, when healthcare organizations operate in a connected, integrated ecosystem, rather than as a standalone entity, they can better engage consumers and solve the pain points that are preventing long-term health.

THE THIRD SHIFT

From Population-Centric
to Person-Centered

Healthcare organizations often focus on creating products, services and experiences for groups of similar consumers, such as those who have the same condition or those who fall into the same demographic. To be truly consumer-centric, it is critical for healthcare organizations to create products, services and experiences for consumers based on their individual needs.

THE FOURTH SHIFT

From Incremental
Improvements to
Pervasive Innovation

Healthcare organizations often settle for small, time-consuming improvements to established systems and processes that were never designed with the consumer in mind. To put the consumer at the center, organizations must reimagine their approach to innovation to truly reinvent the consumer experience. They can consistently adopt both an innovative and a minimally viable product mindset, using a portfolio of approaches to spark wholesale, enterprise-wide change.

THE FIFTH SHIFT

From Insights as a
Department to a Culture of
Consumer Obsession

Establishing insights as a function is critical to gathering intelligence, but it's not enough. Healthcare organizations can go further by creating a culture of consumer obsession, where everyone in the organization always keeps the consumer front and center.

ENABLERS THAT MAKE IT HAPPEN

During our research, we also uncovered two key enablers that will accelerate progress along the five shifts. These enablers will be key to successfully helping organizations implement, scale and sustain the shifts.

ENABLER ONE: Cultural Transformation

As organizations make the shift to consumer centricity, they will need the support of a culture that recognizes and respects the value of the consumer in everything that the organization does. The front desk receptionist, the hourly employee in the call center, the scientist looking for the next breakthrough and the CEO are all critical to a successful transformation and play a role in change management.

ENABLER TWO: Digital Transformation

As organizations work to execute a consumer-centric strategy with supporting tactics, they can shift their view of digital health from a threat to an opportunity for growth. By keeping an open mind, organizations can leverage new technology and digital platforms to transform the experience and improve outcomes.

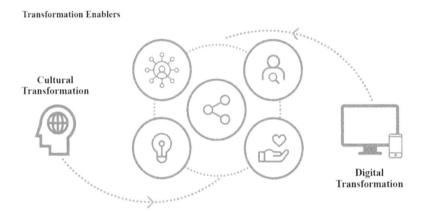

Transformation Enablers

Cultural Transformation

Digital Transformation

WHAT THIS BOOK AIMS TO DO

This book is meant to provide practical advice for leaders who seek to transform the way in which their organizations engage with consumers. In each shift, we paint a picture of what the ideal state is for consumers and outline the key challenges that healthcare organizations face in attempting to achieve that ideal state. We intend this book to be both illustrative and prescriptive, outlining the key steps that healthcare organizations can take to make each shift a reality.

What underpins an organization's ability to transform is its culture, along with the ability to see opportunity in digital health where others see threat and uncertainty. To help organizations establish the key catalysts, we take a similar approach to the enablers as we do for the shifts. We share success stories from organizations that are going through their own transformation—some new companies, some old, but all making progress. While the recency of these stories will fade with time, we believe the shifts and the enablers that they illustrate have a lot of room to run.

We hope these shifts provide organizations with helpful frameworks and examples as they work to achieve this transformation, leading to new growth and reduced costs. More importantly, these shifts empower consumers in the way they deserve and could have a marked improvement on health across the globe. Let's begin *Making the Healthcare Shift*!

The First Shift

From Tactical Fixes to a Holistic Experience Strategy

"At Novant Health, consumer experience is approached holistically. It is built into every strategic touchpoint we have."
–Carl Armato, CEO, Novant Health

The healthcare industry, for the most part, fails to deliver cohesive experiences. Each touchpoint exists independently, and no common thread connects the journey. The experience becomes disjointed and meaningless, making it even more difficult for people to navigate on their own. A burdensome healthcare journey can lead to higher costs and less than optimal health outcomes. To increase connections throughout the journey, organizations can develop a holistic experience strategy to guide the design of experiences under a unifying definition of what consumer centricity means for their organization. That helps connect previously disjointed experiences and ties tactics to a larger holistic experience strategy. Organizations like Apple, Sephora and WeChat win consumers with their innovative and connected experiences, because they start with a holistic, consumer-centric strategy that guides initiatives across the organization.

The First Shift explores the building blocks that must be in place for healthcare organizations to start their transformation. In this chapter, we share how organizations can build the foundation for a definition of consumer centricity and then act on it, building the right team to bring it to life. Before jumping into what healthcare organizations can do to deliver a consumer-centric experience strategy, though, we will share an example from Disney that shows how that organization brought consumer centricity to life in a unified and "magical" way.

LESSON FROM DISNEY: MAKING MAGIC IN MANY TOUCHPOINTS

Disney excels at creating exceptional experiences. The company that gave the world "the happiest place on earth" touches consumers on multiple platforms through many mechanisms. While popularly known for bringing children's favorite fairytale and cartoon characters to life, Disney does far more by creating moments that are relevant to all members of the family and unifying them under a common thread: Bringing magic to life.

From the moment a family decides to make Disney its vacation destination, the organization delivers an impeccable experience. Before departure, families receive MagicBands in the mail, a wearable device that makes the Disney experience seamless by holding dinner reservations, credit-card information and photo storage. Disney takes careful consideration of the small moments that can make or break an experience. Think of the situation in which a parent and child are waiting in line for a ride only to reach the end and discover that the child is too short—or that the expected Epcot dinner reservation cannot be accommodated. Those scenarios would end poorly for Disney and for the families that shell out thousands of dollars for a magical experience. MagicBands put parents in control of their Disney trip, allowing them to schedule in advance, avoid long lines and confirm reservations at their favorite restaurants. MagicBands maximize the chances of magic at every turn and allow Disney to win on two levels: greats odds of keeping families happy and greater data that allows Disney to continuously improve the experience.

Overall, Disney follows two key principles for experience design: First, the company unites all experiences under its "Bringing magic to life" vision. From *Beauty and the Beast* dining halls to easy check-ins at the resort, Disney makes sure there's magic at every touchpoint. Second, Disney views consumers holistically and has a deep understanding of their needs beyond the moment when a child meets Mickey Mouse. Disney recognizes that exceptional experiences are an asset, not an expense. For Disney, the return on investment associated with engaged and loyal consumers always justifies the short-term costs associated with experience design.

CHALLENGE FOR HEALTHCARE: THINKING BEYOND TACTICS

Healthcare is nothing like Walt Disney World. Instead of seamless, personalized and hassle-free moments, consumers endure experiences that are disjointed, frustrating and disconnected from their preferences. In fact, our research with GE Healthcare Partners reveals that 81 percent of consumers are dissatisfied with their healthcare experience; the happiest are those who interact with the system the least. "Many health systems have interpreted consumer centricity to be primarily those face-to-face moments with the doctors, nurses and other care providers. That is when we listen. But where we are falling down is with the systems we have in place that gets patients to those moments with the doctor," says George Sauter, Chief Strategy Officer at John Muir Health. Despite the importance of consumer experience (CX) and the fact that consumers are disappointed with the current state of healthcare, many organizations continue to focus on one-off initiatives like reductions in nighttime noise, better dining options and more efficient parking instead of creating a cohesive journey aligned with a broad strategy. While those initiatives solve specific consumer pain points, they only serve as a Band-Aid. "Historically, we had so many separate initiatives to address different pain points that it was actually diluting the focus on the consumer. We needed to determine one consistent, holistic journey," says Natalie Schneider, Vice President of Customer Experience at Anthem, the American health insurer.

In publicly funded systems such as the U.K.'s National Health Service, this problem is exacerbated due to limited capacity and aging populations. "If you look at the U.K. system, we don't typically look after individuals and manage their requirements over a lifetime. We identify a problem, seek out a solution, say thank you and goodbye… who's next?" says Peter Corfield, Chief Commercial Officer at Spire Healthcare Group, a private healthcare provider in the United Kingdom. As a private entity in a public system, Corfield believes that creating a cohesive, holistic consumer experience is a great opportunity. "When we talk about a proper consumer experience, we're not just talking about medical training or caregiving," he says. "We're also talking about making it easier for consumers, recognizing where they are coming from and seeking to develop a long-term relationship."

The healthcare journey is complex, and many different stakeholders are involved—which makes it difficult for healthcare organizations to address the entire experience. "You have to think about your customers, whoever they may be, more holistically and less transactionally," says Dennis Murphy, CEO of Indiana University Health. "When people come to our healthcare system, they aren't touching us just once. They're touching us many times over an extended period. You have to understand the entirety of their experience. How well it's connected and how seamless it is drives satisfaction and engagement as any individual experience." The problem of creating fragmented experiences is likely driven by the fact that healthcare organizations often measure success through touchpoint feedback. In fact, 71 percent of the organizations we surveyed report relying on experience-satisfaction scores (e.g., appointment satisfaction) or touchpoint metrics (e.g., waiting-room time) to evaluate how well an organization is delivering. While this type of measurement works for touchpoint optimization, it leads to addressing consumer pain points in a disjointed manner. "Customer experience is more than just touchpoints that roll up into journeys. It's the series of experiences over time that define the overall relationship with an organization," says Charlene Li, Principal Analyst at Altimeter, Prophet's digital research company, and author of "Experience Strategy: Connecting Customer Experience to Business Strategy." Healthcare organizations can easily claim they are consumer-centric, but the execution of their strategies frequently lacks the necessary support.

SOLUTION: UNITED UNDER A SINGLE EXPERIENCE STRATEGY

Instead of focusing efforts on touchpoints, organizations should unify the entire journey under an overarching experience strategy. Nearly half of the organizations that we surveyed report being in the beginning stages of the First Shift, suggesting that they understand the need to optimize experience touchpoints but lack a plan for bringing it all together. Organizations need to define what consumer centricity means for them and allow that to inform a holistic experience strategy, clarifying goals and tactics to successfully activate it.

Here are ways for organizations to get started:

- Define consumer centricity for the organization in a way that is consistent with the business model and organizational strategy.
- Codify the definition of consumer centricity so it can be socialized and activated across the business.
- Develop a roadmap of initiatives that will deliver a consumer-centric experience and identify bold moves that will jump-start momentum.
- Build a strong organizational engine with the appropriate structure and expertise to deliver the holistic experience.

Here Are Ways Organizations Can Get Started:

1	2	3	4
Define consumer centricity for the organization in a way that is consistent with the business model and organizational strategy	*Codify the definition of consumer centricity so it can be socialized and activated across the business*	*Develop a roadmap of initiatives that will deliver a consumer-centric experience and identify bold moves that will jump-start momentum*	*Build a strong organizational engine with the right structure and expertise to deliver the holistic experience*

SYNCHRONIZE CONSUMER CENTRICITY AND THE BUSINESS MODEL

While many healthcare organizations have woven consumer centricity into written missions or visions, leaders tell us that translating consumer centricity into a living, organizational strategy is challenging—fully realizing that a consumer-centric strategy requires significant changes to overall mindsets, organizational structure, employee incentives and investment priorities. Once an organization has determined what consumer centricity will mean for it, a critical step is determining if the business is, in fact, designed to deliver on it.

LESSON FROM INTERMOUNTAIN HEALTHCARE: GO AHEAD. BREAK YOUR BUSINESS MODEL.

This is what Utah's Intermountain Healthcare did. Given recent healthcare reform, Intermountain saw the writing on the wall. "We recognized that traditional modes of healthcare, where we wait until people are ill just to treat them in our facilities, were not serving our patients or our customers in the way that we need to serve them," says Dan Liljenquist, Vice President of Enterprise Initiative Office at Intermountain.

Changes within the industry pushed Intermountain to re-evaluate whether its current mission, which also serves as its vision of being "a model healthcare system," could lead to success. After deliberation and debate, the organization decided to change its mission to help people "live the healthiest lives." The problem, though, was that the system was designed to carry out the previous mission, not the new one. Hospitals were the heartbeat of Intermountain Healthcare. The system had a traditional hospital- and facility-based care model and even owned its payer network and medical group in order to drive additional volume to its own hospitals. And it had developed a medical group to direct additional volume into the hospitals. This model meant that the majority of the system's margin was generated by hospitals, making it challenging to deliver on a mission that was instead focused on the health of the population. The two strategies clashed: One aimed to keep hospitals full and efficient, and the other aimed to keep people out of the hospitals. "When the weight of your organization is on the facility model, it's really tough to disrupt yourself. So we took a page out of Clayton Christensen's book and recognized that we're not going to transform if we conflate two business models," says Liljenquist.

In 2017, to address the conflicting models, Intermountain restructured into two areas. One consists of specialists, primarily oriented around the hospitals; this area was focused on getting the lowest cost per case and determining how to get the best value on care given at its facilities. The system also split the medical group in half, creating a community-based care group aimed at per-member and per-month cost reduction. The focus for this second area became engagement outside the facilities, medication adherence and identification of health problems before they become critical. This restructuring ensures that the community-based care group is fully engaged, both economically and clinically, in keeping people well and out of facilities.

Intermountain Healthcare understood that consumer centricity wasn't possible without a business model that supports it in a real way. "Like many places, even as mission-driven and community focused as we've been, we also have been pretty provider-centric. If we want to make our transition to consumer centricity possible, we will need to disrupt ourselves," says CEO Marc Harrison, M.D. When healthcare organizations take on consumer centricity, they need to consider its viability given their current business model. If an organization's definition of consumer centricity and its business model are not in harmony, the organization will be unable to move forward. Of course, splitting the organization in two is not realistic for most organizations; the strategic intent, however, should be.

WORDS MATTER: CODIFY CONSUMER CENTRICITY DEFINITION

Another way in which organizations can define what consumer centricity will look like for them is by codifying the term in an easily digestible manner. Organizations can clarify and articulate consumer centricity in a way that is both actionable and compelling and also helps guide the experience. Since everyone has a role in delivering consumer experiences, organizations need to give each employee a clear understanding of the strategy. We suggest creating experience principles and guidelines that describe how the organization wants consumers to feel throughout the journey. Words like empathy, compassion and feelings are words that are not often used to define experiences in healthcare; but they must become the norm when developing principles that will lead to the design of consumer-centric experiences. For simplicity's sake, we encourage developing no more than five principles.

LEARN FROM PIEDMONT HEALTHCARE: WHAT'S YOUR MANIFESTO?

To succeed in a highly competitive environment, Piedmont knew it needed to reimagine the consumer experience both to increase consideration and selection among consumers and to unify the organization around a common brand experience. The result of this effort was the "Piedmont Way," a manifesto guiding all aspects of the patient experience. Through interviews, consumer research and extensive site visits, Piedmont developed five key principles. The system even wrote a statement about the organization's vision. "At Piedmont Healthcare, we are all in this for one reason—to make a difference in every life we touch. From our front lines to our back office and everywhere in between, we are all caregivers, working together behind the scenes to make you feel important and cared for. That means giving you our individual attention and using every resource, human and digital, to seamlessly connect the dots across your healthcare journey. At Piedmont Healthcare, we have one priority: genuinely delivering genuinely good care. That's our way, The Piedmont Way." Piedmont's five experience principles support this mission: Lead With Human, Connect the Journey, Anticipate Needs, Create Uplifting Moments and Enrich With Technology.

These principles will create system alignment and guide new products, services and training design that support cultural change and will help in the development of service standards and behavioral guidelines. "We've defined patient experience for the organization," says Katie Logan, Vice President of Experience. "It's a part of our strategy, our strategic imperatives and the plan on the page that gets shared across the organization as our direction. We have a set of principles that tell us 'What?' and a set of tactics that tell us 'How?'"

Piedmont Healthcare's Experience Principles

1		Lead with Human
2		Connect the Journey
3		Anticipate Needs
4		Create Uplifting Moments
5		Enrich with Technology

Piedmont HEALTHCARE

JUMP-START WITH BOLD MOVES

To truly deliver on consumer centricity, organizations need to make deliberate moves. In one of our discussions, we heard from a leader of a prominent American health insurer that, when it first committed to consumer centricity, nothing much happened. There was nothing to galvanize the organization to act. Our research uncovered the ways in which healthcare organizations can effectively push themselves into action by making bold declarations.

LEARN FROM GEISINGER HEALTH: PUT MONEY ON THE LINE

When David Feinberg, M.D., became CEO of Geisinger Health System, a regional health system in Pennsylvania, he shifted the organization's focus to the consumer experience. Within his first year at the organization, he told *Becker's Hospital Review* that his ultimate goal was "eliminating the waiting room and everything it represents. A waiting room means we're provider-centered—it means the doctor is the most important person and everyone is on their time."[31]

"We began to ask, 'How can we make it so, when people step into a hospital, they don't feel like they stepped into a hospital?'" says Geisinger Chief Informatics Officer Alistair Erskine, M.D. Geisinger set an aggressive goal of achieving a Net Promoter Score (NPS) in the top 10 percent of all brands, which would require it to move from its current score of 24 to nearly 50. If that was going to work, patient experience needed to become a top priority—and quickly.

But making that change required a seismic shift in the way the organization interacted with patients. Words could take them only so far. "Everyone talks about putting the patient first, and that's great— but to make it actually happen, we needed to take a big step that would force us to change," says Dr. Erskine. If Geisinger wanted to truly become consumer-centric, it needed to signal to consumers and employees alike that consumers were a priority. To accomplish that, Geisinger announced ProvenExperience, a refund program with a

---

31   https://www.beckershospitalreview.com/hospital-management-administration/
     the-corner-office-dr-david-feinberg-on-raising-the-patient-experience-to-a-whole-
     new-level.html

special app that allowed patients to easily provide feedback on their experiences and receive refunds on their copays for poor experiences. Within a year of launching the program, Geisinger had refunded nearly $500,000 to patients. ProvenExperience galvanized the organization to operate with the consumer at the center of everything it does and to demonstrate to patients that the hospital system trusts and values feedback. "The point is not so much the money part. It's about signaling that 'Look, we put our trust in you, the patient, because you've put your trust in us,'" Dr. Erskine says. In addition to media coverage, ProvenExperience provides Geisinger with valuable data on common pain points across the journey, as well as the ability to measure the impact of solutions. With a holistic understanding of pain points along the journey, Geisinger can address them in a unified way that is consistent with its definition of consumer centricity. And by putting money on the line, Geisinger has elevated consumer centricity from an idea to a movement.

SEEK DIGITAL DOMINANCE

Other organizations are also taking small, deliberate steps like this to move their organizations in the right direction. Georgia's Piedmont Healthcare, for example, launched several initiatives—from virtual visits and online scheduling to physician ratings and reviews—in order to propel the organization forward. "If you don't put a stake in the ground and tell everyone, 'This is what our consumer requires of us, so we're going to go after it and succeed,' it can be very difficult to get people on board," says Chief Consumer Officer Matt Gove.

Intermountain Healthcare is also using a bold approach, laying out deliberate steps to be "the first digitally-enabled, consumer-centric, integrated delivery system." Dr. Harrison explains that the health system's plan focuses on cost reduction, digital integration and access, as well as how those initiatives will move the organization forward. "We're taking cues from Amazon, financial technology companies, Starbucks and the like. We are going to inject that holistically into a real digital transformation of an integrated health system to truly understand and serve people the way they want to be served," Dr. Harrison says. And Intermountain is putting the funding of consumer centricity at the heart of its health system.

BUILD THE RIGHT TEAM

Of course, these efforts are only as strong as the team responsible for bringing them to life and for moving the organization along with its transformation. Consumer-centric organizations are often led by individuals with a CX-first mindset. While those leaders come with an array of important credentials, the most effective tend to have a blended background in healthcare, strategy or consumer-centric industries. Through discussions with healthcare executives, three CX leader archetypes emerged that are all ready to drive change: The Invested Healer, The Best-Practice Strategist and The Lifelong Consumerist. While each of those leader types can play an effective role, the most effective teams blend them all.

- **The Invested Healer** Leaders with a background in medicine or clinical care, they have hands-on experience working with patients, deeply understand the clinical experience and have a personal interest in improving the overall patient experience
- **The Best-Practice Strategist** These leaders come from industries like consulting, where they have worked with organizations in many sectors to solve a range of business challenges similar to those in healthcare
- **The Lifelong Consumerist** Experts from consumer-centric industries, such as packaged goods, bring a consumer-first mindset

Archetypes of CX Leaders

THE INVESTED HEALER	**THE BEST-PRACTICE STRATEGIST**	**THE LIFELONG CONSUMERIST**
With a background in medicine or clinical care, they have hands-on experience working with patients, deeply understand the clinical experience and have a personal interest in improving the overall patient experience	These leaders come from industries like consulting, where they have worked with organizations in many sectors to solve a range of business challenges similar to those in healthcare	Experts from consumer-centric industries, such as packaged goods, bring a consumer-first mindset

The Invested Healer: Prakash Patel, M.D.

Invested Healers tend to bring a different level of credibility and authority to the conversation due to their clinical or medical background. These leaders have both owned and delivered the experience. The biggest challenge that Invested Healers face is not being able to draw from a portfolio of outside experiences, which mandates that they surround themselves with a leadership team that brings balance to the role. One such leader is Florida Blue's Chief Operating Officer and Guidewell Health's President Prakash Patel, M.D. With training from Weill Cornell Medical College, Dr. Patel understands the ins and outs of the healthcare industry and is committed to building experiences that provide quality care. Intent on bringing a highly personalized touch to the way in which health insurance is delivered, he led the development of programs like Florida Blue's Place of Delivery Teams, which combine multidisciplinary clinical and nonclinical teams working on a local basis and even directly meeting patients and providers. "We are interfacing in a much more hands-on, integrated environment with customers and their providers," he says. "We want to do something different than the old paradigm of having a centralized call center." With his prior experience serving patients in the clinic, Dr. Patel understands the importance of the human touch in all aspects of healthcare, including insurance.

The Best-Practice Strategist: Dave Edelman

Best-Practice Strategists are leaders who come from business and/or consulting backgrounds and have worked across many industries to deliver world-class consumer experiences. These leaders have had the benefit of seeing what has and has not worked in a myriad of outside categories and can incorporate best practices, tailoring them to healthcare. As a former management consultant, Aetna's CMO Dave Edelman has extensive experience working with companies in an array of industries, helping them implement new strategies and processes. Leaders like Edelman bring a strategic perspective to healthcare and are skilled at introducing models from different industries. This kind of thinking led Edelman to adapt Spotify's innovation framework for Aetna: Cross-functional teams work together as startups to bring new ideas to life. Before Aetna, Edelman used this method with his clients and, because of his implementation experience, it's working at Aetna, too. "We get cross-functional teams together in war rooms to focus and get stuff moving with fast, iterative cycles," he says. "These test-and-learns are powered by data."

The Lifelong Consumerist: Jill Chandor

Lifelong Consumerists often bring the richest experiences by operating CX in diverse categories, but these leaders are usually furthest away from the practice of healthcare; so getting complimentary healthcare knowledge and leadership alignment is critical. Jill Chandor, Division Chair of Brand Strategy and Creative Studio for the Mayo Clinic, spent nearly 20 years in the fiercely competitive retail banking business before switching to healthcare. Leaders like Chandor bring a reflexive instinct of "patients as consumers" and a new perspective. These leaders understand the power of insights, know the importance of experiences and content and push new thinking. "Healthcare insiders know almost too much and need to remember that their own compelling reasons to believe are often quite different from those that resonate with consumers," Chandor says. "Having an outsider's perspective helps you inspire simple, relevant messages founded in consumer research even if they are not motivating to healthcare professionals individually."

LEARN FROM MOUNT SINAI HEALTH SYSTEM: WIN WITH CROSS-FUNTIONAL LEADERSHIP

While each of these types of leaders adds credibility and experience, it is important to remember that cross-functional engagement and leadership typically make the strongest team. By building a group of leaders across functions and departments, healthcare organizations can ensure that consumer centricity starts at the top. Kenneth Davis, M.D., President and CEO of Mount Sinai Health System, fits the Invested Healer archetype and has made patient satisfaction and patient-centered care a critical issue in his system. "It took decades for the culture to change to put the patient first rather than the physician," he says in an interview with *Modern Healthcare*.[32] "The marketplace in Manhattan is the most competitive on Earth. Now there is a necessity to be patient-centered." As the leader at Mount Sinai, Dr. Davis has built a team to change the organization's culture and strategy. In 2015, he hired Niyum Gandhi as Executive Vice President and Chief Population Officer to oversee Mount Sinai's transition from a primarily fee-for-service model to an approach inclusive of value and risk-based population health. Gandhi fits the Best-Practice Strategist archetype, having come

---

32   http://www.modernhealthcare.com/article/20160820/MAGAZINE/308209955

from a management consulting background where he served as a partner in the Health and Life Sciences practice and focused on value-based healthcare transformation. To lead marketing, Dr. Davis hired Margaret Coughlin as Senior Vice President, Chief Marketing and Communications Officer, in 2017. She fits the Lifelong Consumerist archetype, starting her career at Procter & Gamble and in the advertising agency world. Together, the team is poised to drive transformation through a relentless focus on understanding and delivering on consumers' needs from three important perspectives.

ESTABLISH THE RIGHT ORGANIZATIONAL STRUCTURE

Some find that their historical organization-chart structure hinders the success of consumer centricity. To thrive, the positioning of consumer-centricity teams is important. And no matter where they sit in the organization chart, they need strong, clear connections to the CEO and also need to be well respected and supported. In our research, we uncovered three ways in which CX teams can be successful:

CX Lives Under Marketing: At Aetna, CX is part of the Marketing Department. This works at Aetna, because marketing is seen as essential to strategic decisions. Marketing can deliver quick wins to build credibility, or the organization can invest in the marketing team through a strategic hire—as Aetna did with Dave Edelman.

A Separate CX Team: Piedmont Healthcare has a centralized CX team comprised of cross-service line players within the Physician Enterprise Group. This elevates the importance of CX within the organization. Katie Logan, VP of Experience at Piedmont Healthcare, says that having her team sit within the Physician Enterprise Group is important, since executing much of the consumer-centric strategy requires the support and cooperation of physicians and their operations. "We are laying the foundation for some of these pieces and how we will execute and implement them," she says. "We want to deploy [CX] across the entire organization with some level of consistency; and by starting at the top of the funnel, we can work our way through the customer journey."

A Decentralized Team: Like many other organizations, biotechnology company Amgen has a dedicated patient engagement team focused on consistently incorporating the voice of the patient throughout the value chain. However, the organization believes the most impact happens through a decentralized model supported by the appropriate accountability and incentives. "The real change that we believe the organization needs, is to be decentralized," says Jessica Nora, Amgen's Executive Director of Patient Engagement Strategy, "so we have a group of patient centricity leaders, which are high potential executive directors and directors, sponsored by their vice presidents." These dedicated leads sit across the organization to ensure the patient voice is being elevated and represented across functions and regions. They are responsible for developing a patient centricity network within their functions and making progress against specific goals. "For us, the decentralized team made the most sense, but we understand we have to be disciplined about it," says Jessica. "If you are going to have a decentralized model you have to set goals or establish incentives that everyone aligns on, at the start. This is so critical."

Making the shift to a holistic consumer experience strategy will jump-start an organization's transition to

Archetypes of Consumer Experience Org Structure

#		Description
1		**CX Lives Under Marketing**
2		**A Separate CX Team**
3		**A Decentralized Team**

consumer centricity. It sets the stage for the other shifts to come and helps distill the commitment to change. The process of making consumer centricity a strategic priority is complex, so let's review some key takeaways from The First Shift:

Align the Definition of Consumer Centricity With the Business Model

In a world that is increasingly moving to value-based reimbursement, healthcare organizations may find that their businesses are not designed to encourage consumer centricity. Like Intermountain Healthcare, organizations need to ensure that the way they make money and run the business enables consumer centricity. What is the organizational structure today? Does it allow the organization flexibility to deliver on consumer centricity?

Put Pen to Paper

To ensure that employees understand consumer centricity, organizations can codify principles that will guide consumer-centric experience development like the Piedmont Way guides the Piedmont experience. Those principles should help employees articulate what consumer centricity means for the strategy as a whole and what it means for how they should approach their jobs each day.

Make Bold Moves for Progress

Many healthcare organizations support consumer centricity; but until they make concerted efforts that push the organization to act, that goal can never be realized. Organizations need to consider making bold moves that inspire action and ignite change the way Geisinger's ProvenExperience did for its system. Where are the biggest opportunities for signaling change that will involve employees across the organization? Can this bold move work for mobilizing the business internally and engaging consumers externally?

Assemble the Dream Team

Organizations need to ensure that they have a strong leadership team in place and the right structure to enable a consumer-centric strategy. Organizations can analyze their leaders that are already in place and identify each one as an *Invested Healer*, a *Best Practice Strategist* or a *Life-Long Consumerist*. Do those leaders have the support they need to successfully lead consumer centricity efforts? And does the organizational structure empower those leaders and help them drive consumer centricity across the organization?

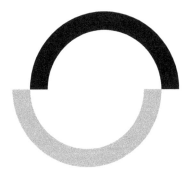

The Second Shift

From Fragmented Care to Connected Ecosystems

"I cannot be responsible for population health if I am waiting for those three hours a year when I interact with a patient. I have to consider how to extend my influence and show up differently."

**—John Haney, Area Vice President Southeast,
Johnson & Johnson (former VP, Healthcare Strategic Marketing)**

Healthcare journeys are frustrating and fragmented, making engagement and health outcomes difficult to improve. "The system is so fragmented," says Jeffrey Dachis, CEO of One Drop, "it is a burden on patients and is incredibly disempowering." Consumers are responsible for managing connections between their many providers, their health plan and their pharmacy. Even more damaging, treatment plans fail to consider the many factors that influence a consumer's health, leading to suboptimal outcomes. To do better, healthcare organizations can imitate the approach of companies like Peloton or Spotify, which focus on developing solutions that package discrete parts of the journey in a single offering without requiring the consumer to do it themselves.

In the Second Shift, we explore how organizations can move from fragmented care to connected ecosystems. Let's start with the story of MyFitnessPal, which has evolved from a calorie-counting platform to a full health approach—one that focuses on solutions rather than products.

LEARN FROM MYFITNESSPAL: THINK BEYOND THE BASICS

When Mike and Albert Lee launched the first MyFitnessPal app in 2009, their goal was to make weight management, through calorie tracking, easier. Since then, the platform has grown into an integrated health and wellness solution; and in 2015, athletic wear company Under Armor bought MyFitnessPal, integrating Under Armor tracking tools and broadening the platform's geographic reach.[33] The value of MyFitnessPal is its holistic approach to healthy living that addresses the many ways that one stays healthy—from nutrition to exercise and weight management—and the barriers that stand in consumers' way. MyFitnessPal knows that many consumers are unaware of the nutritional and caloric value of the food they consume; so the platform curates a vast database of foods, which helps users make better decisions and tracks their behavior. For other people, cooking is a significant obstacle to health management; so MyFitnessPal has a recipe platform for sharing healthy recipes, inspiring others.

---

33   https://www.statista.com/statistics/650748/health-fitness-app-usage-usa/

MyFitnessPal also understands that many consumers are motivated by community; so the platform includes an online community where individuals can work toward a common goal, share their experiences and frustration and seek advice from others.

The MyFitnessPal platform also syncs data from a variety of apps. While some of those apps, such as MapMyRun are owned by Under Armor, the majority are created by other organizations such as Strava, iWatch and Fitbit. MyFitnessPal is open to collaborating with these outsiders, because its focus is to drive engagement—not push products. Although MyFitnessPal faces the risks and challenges of data-heavy companies, it has become a remarkable platform of integrated services and solutions that gives users a holistic view of their health. The value of this complete platform and experience is priceless, as it solves a wide range of pain points and makes achieving a healthier lifestyle easier. When MyFitnessPal first launched, the intention was not to build such a platform but, rather, to be a "point solution" standing on its own and filling a very specific need. But as consumer engagement became more important to holistic health success, MyFitnessPal leaned on a mix of strategy, agility and consumer insight to build a brand that is now considered a category of one.

CHALLENGE FOR HEALTHCARE: CONNECTING THE BROKEN PIECES

A connected healthcare journey seems unimaginable, because healthcare organizations still struggle to reduce fragmentation within their own organizations let alone handle service gaps in the broader industry. Healthcare provider systems, struggling to maintain even minimal connection with the various physicians on a patient's care team, are a prime example. Quite often, specialists do not communicate with primary-care doctors, and administrations of specialty clinics don't communicate with each other. And as healthcare has become more siloed, the situation has gotten worse. "Independent decision making led to independent experiences, which led to industry fragmentation that has only deepened," says Kevin Brown, CEO of Piedmont Healthcare.

Fragmentation hinders the development of solutions both inside organizations and in their outside collaborations. Providers like Kaiser Permanente, Intermountain Healthcare or Geisinger Health System that have built integrated delivery networks from the ground up are an obvious exception, as they started with a strong cultural foundation that encourages both integration and coordination with the consumer at the center. Historically, though, healthcare organizations have not developed solutions that address variables outside the clinic and how the intersection of those variables impacts a person's health. Healthcare organizations typically limit services to those that are in their direct line of sight and responsibility. Providers perform tests and procedures, pharma companies develop and sell drugs and insurers manage financial transactions. As a result, the healthcare industry delivers a fragmented journey, where patients are expected to manage their health on their own and act as the liaison between and among provider, payer and pharmacy. "Patients are tired of navigating the system on their own. They are sick and tired of the healthcare system— it's fragmented, painful, confusing, costly," says GuideWell's Dr. Patel. This frustration not only affects health outcomes, but it's also bad for business. Our research with healthcare consumers at a large Midwestern provider revealed that better coordination of care is a key driver of selection of one provider over another.

If healthcare organizations want to engage patients in a way that reduces costs and improves outcomes, those organizations need to go beyond their traditional responsibilities, create a solution-oriented mindset and serve consumers in ways not seen before in healthcare.

The Healthcare Ecosystem

FIND SOLUTIONS IN THE CONSUMER'S WORLD

A solution-oriented mindset requires understanding the healthcare ecosystem—all the factors and stakeholders that influence health—and connecting those factors in order to create solutions that engage consumers in ways that are both seamless and reminiscent of the experiences they're having in other areas of their life. Unfortunately, most healthcare organizations typically focus on providing single products, services or experiences; but the efficacy of those offerings depends on the factors and environment that surround them. "You have to understand the consumer's world, not just when they're a patient. It's not just about when they're in a paper gown. Health systems need to understand the patient's preferences and expectations outside this environment," says Kevin Kumler, President of Health Systems at Zocdoc, an online medical-care scheduling company.

Through our discussions with healthcare leaders, we determined that organizations need to move away from simply addressing a single pain point or developing a new product or service touchpoint and, instead, start moving toward offering fully integrated solutions. Connecting the factors of an ecosystem is no easy task, and the majority of healthcare organizations are just starting the process. This shift is more challenging for payers than for other players, and 68 percent of payers report that they are only in the beginning stages. This lag is likely because payers have historically existed with just one role, so connecting to the healthcare ecosystem requires payer organizations to rethink the part they play within the healthcare system.

"PLUS PRODUCT" SOLUTIONS ENGAGE CUSTOMERS

To make this transition, we propose working from a model we first heard about from Jean-Michel Cossery, former VP of Oncology North America at Eli Lilly and Co. That model outlines three types of offers that an organization can make to consumers. The first is *Product,* a stand-alone drug, service or plan. The primary objective of this *Product* offering is to push the product, which consumers then learn to use on their own. The second is a *Product Plus*, which means the single drug, service or plan is enhanced with "wraparound" services such as educational materials, patient-support programs or digital tools such as an app. The primary objective of *Product Plus* is still to push the product; but at this stage, and at the most basic level, the organization assists the consumer in using the product. The third offering, called a *Plus Product,* takes a comprehensive solution-oriented approach to serving the patient—layering on elements, as needed, to create an ecosystem and drive the desired outcome. The primary objective of the *Plus Product* is to engage the consumers, guide them through the journey and build a relationship with them. Organizations that want to increase consumer engagement should aim to build *Plus Products*.

Developing *Plus* Product Solutions

Product	**Product *Plus***	***Plus* Product**
Drug, service or plan is the primary product	Drug, service or plan comes with "wrap around" services	Drug, service or plan is part of a "solution" ecosystem package

Plus Product solutions are standard practice for companies outside of healthcare. For example, when Apple first launched the iPhone in 2007, it partnered with AT&T as its network provider. Instead of sending consumers down the street to deal with the AT&T sign-up experience, Apple consumers could set up phones in its store, using "geniuses" to help them through the process. Apple went beyond the typical role of the phone manufacturer and connected with the consumer by eliminating what is often a tedious experience for consumers.

Getting to *Plus Product* requires:

- Building a thorough, deep understanding of consumer pain points.

- Understanding other players within the healthcare ecosystem that can help address the pain points and develop a holistic solution.
- Aligning with a willingness to collaborate across business silos. The components of a *Plus Product* often fall outside the walls of a single organization, requiring coordination and partnership.

Once an organization determines the components and necessary partnerships required to succeed, it will be better equipped to create offerings that engage and empower consumers.

MOVING TO PLUS PRODUCT TAKES FORTITUDE

Getting Started

The first step in developing a *Plus Product* solution is identifying the barriers that consumers face in trying to stay healthy. This step requires an understanding of consumer pain points and a willingness to invest in solving them. Of course, consumers face several different pain points and barriers throughout the healthcare journey; so organizations can prioritize those pain points and barriers according to their greatest business and consumer impact.

Once an organization has determined its consumer pain points, it should consider how to develop solutions starting from the eyes of the consumer. Some of those pain points will be common across all consumer groups, but the solutions to overcoming them will likely differ. For example, adopting a healthier diet is a common challenge for diabetics of any age, socioeconomic class or education level; but the solutions will vary across those groups. For working moms, the greatest hurdle may be lack of time to invest in nutrition research or meal prep; for low-income mothers, the barrier is even greater due to the lack of money. Those obstacles are complex, and organizations should be sensitive to their nuances when developing solutions. We have found that organizations are often better equipped to account for the differences when they explore solutions at a local level.

After an organization determines its *Plus Product* solution, the organization needs to consider the resources necessary to build the ecosystem. Health organizations can either build, buy or rent in order to successfully offer their own version of *Plus Product*. There are merits to each approach; and depending on both internal capabilities and the required speed of execution, any of the approaches may prove effective. Geisinger Health, for example, internally built a nutritional program that supports local communities. And pharmaceutical company Roche acquired digital platforms, like diabetes-care management company mySugr, after years of partnership. Other organizations, such as AIA and Vitality, choose partnership.

When surveyed about the roadblocks that prevent *Plus Product* thinking, healthcare leaders cite a spectrum of problems ranging from talent and budget to internal silos and regulatory measures. To overcome those roadblocks, organizations like Mount Sinai Health and Boehringer Ingelheim entered into partnerships, which we will explore later, that rely on the respective strengths of each party to create integrated solutions.

Build, Buy, or Rent?

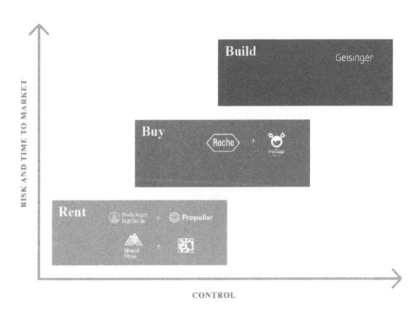

The following examples illustrate how organizations have used a variety of internal capabilities and external partnerships to create solutions for consumers that engage them and produce better outcomes. We explore how Mount Sinai Health System collaborated with a local labor union to develop a total joint replacement solution in order to help ease the burden of that surgery on patients. We also discuss how Geisinger Healthcare opened a food pharmacy to serve low-income diabetic patients. Finally, we examine how Blue Cross Blue Shield of Massachusetts, Boehringer Ingelheim and the U.K.'s National Health Service each use technology partnerships to design solution packages for their consumers.

LEARN FROM MOUNT SINAI: IDENTIFY WHERE CONSUMERS GET STUCK

In 2015, New York's Mount Sinai Health System partnered with the 32BJ Health Fund, which provides benefits to members of the U.S.'s largest union of property service workers, to co-design a bundled Total Joint Replacement (TJR) package with amenities that address common challenges that patients face. The two organizations understood that given the complexity of the operation and its burden on patients, they needed to connect the ecosystem with a Plus-Product solution.

The Health Fund understood that TJR surgeries can be challenging for its members: coordinating resources for a successful surgery and recovery can be difficult. To uncover specific challenges related to TJR, 32BJ conducted comprehensive focus groups with its members. The research revealed that members lacked important information and navigation assistance to ensure a healthy recovery. Patients did have access to information about what they needed for a healthy recovery, or how they could be prepare for their recovery. As a result, many patients incorrectly believed that they would need to recover in a skilled nursing facility.

Consumer-First Solutions

The *Product Plus* solution that the hospital and the Health Fund created was designed specifically to meet the needs of the Fund's members. With such a narrow focus, the two organizations could be precise and targeted. The final bundle program for TJR includes additional services that address the key challenges identified in the research. The hospital system provides a care guide to work, one-on-one, with patients from the day they schedule the surgery through their recovery. The care guides act as advocates and help members understand how to take care of themselves during their recovery period.

To help members during their recovery, the Fund waives copays on the first 10 physical therapy visits within the first 50 days after discharge. The final component the TJR surgery bundled package, known as a reference price, pushes patients to go to settings that are at or under the reference price of joint replacement surgery in the Mount Sinai program. "When we looked at this procedure, we saw where the gaps were; and we believe it's our responsibility to fill those for the patient, using the entire ecosystem at hand" says Lucas Pauls, Plan Sponsor Channel Lead, who helped manage the partnership.

Leveraging Strengths

Given the various components of the *Plus Product* solution, the Fund and Mount Sinai leveraged their unique strengths to share the investment and logistics of the solution. Because of the Fund's trusted relationships with members, the two organizations determined that the Fund would provide no-cost physical therapy as an incentive for members to use the program. Given the hospital's medical expertise and deep understanding of the healthcare system, Mount Sinai took responsibility for providing the patient navigation. Combining their expertise led to an efficient and successful program that addresses TJR in its entirety, not just the operation itself.

Lower Costs, Happier Patients

Within the first year of the program, Mount Sinai, 32BJ and patients experienced improved outcomes and lower costs. Patients reported high satisfaction with their experience, and the number of skilled nursing facility discharges dropped by 12 percentage points. In addition to improved health outcomes, the reference price on the TJR surgeries led to a four-fold increase in the volume of TJR surgeries at Mount Sinai. Because members sought out more reasonably priced hospitals, the program led to nearly $13,000 in savings per operation switched to Mount Sinai. By considering the broader care journey and speaking directly with patients about their needs, organizations can create added value that produces win-win situations. At Mount Sinai, care became far more than just the procedure; rather, it was about the many additional factors shaping recovery. In the future, Mount Sinai plans to expand similar offerings to all TJR services and design similar programs for other procedures.

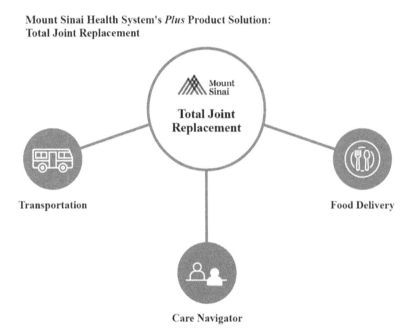

Mount Sinai Health System's *Plus* Product Solution:
Total Joint Replacement

LEARN FROM GEISINGER HEALTH: WRITE AN Rx FOR FOOD, NOT MEDICATION

One disease state where *Plus Product* solutions have had a profound impact is diabetes. While it is true that diabetes is often considered a global epidemic, diabetes can be appropriately managed with preventative measures and medication. Problems arise when the condition is not managed properly or proactively. Take, for example,

Pennsylvania resident Tom Shicowich, who shared the story of his uncontrolled Type 2 diabetes with NPR in 2017.[34] Tom developed an infection in his toe which he initially suspected was flu-related. Instead, within in 24 hours, Tom found himself in the hospital for an amputation and two weeks of intravenous antibiotics. The total cost of Tom's care was nearly $200,000, $23,000 of which he paid out of pocket. A single preventable incident caused Tom enormous physical and financial injury. These occurrences are not uncommon in the United States or around the world. In fact, a 2016 joint study led by scientists at Imperial College London, Harvard T. H. Chan School of Public Health and the World Health Organization estimates that the annual global healthcare costs related to diabetes are nearly $825 billion—yet many of these costs are preventable.[35]

Pennsylvania's Geisinger Health System is all too familiar with the costs associated with diabetes and took on the challenge of tackling this public-health issue. Geisinger Health understood that the biggest challenge for improving and sustaining health among diabetic patients was not something that could be solved with medication alone; rather, it required a change in behavior. Geisinger Health identified that consumers who struggle the most with behavioral change are low-income, food-insecure consumers. Those people have limited access to, and are unable to afford, nutritious, fresh foods that help slow or reverse the progression of the disease. To tackle this challenge, Geisinger Health designed the Fresh Food Pharmacy.

This "pharmacy" looks less like a traditional pharmacy and more like a grocery store. The shelves are stocked with healthy staples like

---

34   https://www.npr.org/sections/thesalt/2017/05/08/526952657/fresh-food-by-prescription-this-health-care-firm-is-trimming-costs-and-waistline

35   https://www.hsph.harvard.edu/news/press-releases/diabetes-cost-825-billion-a-year/

whole-grain pasta and beans; refrigerators hold fresh produce, low-fat dairy, meats and fish. This pharmacy is not just for grocery shopping; it also serves as an educational lab, where participants learn from registered dietitians how to prepare recipes and adopt eating habits that lead to a healthy lifestyle. After their visit, participants go home with a "prescription" of five days' worth of free, fresh food. This program addresses the two major pain points for adopting a healthier lifestyle: money and education. Instead of receiving a potentially outdated or irrelevant pamphlet on healthy living, participants get hands-on personalized guidance for changing lifestyle habits. The Fresh Food Pharmacy program targets low-income patients, so providing free food solves the financial burden. "If we really want to control diabetes, we need to remove obstacles for our patients. And providing free, healthy food costs a lot less than the cost of treating complications from diabetes, including cardiovascular disease, nerve and foot damage, eye problems, kidney disease," says Houssam Abdul-Al, M.D., the primary-care physician treating patients in the program, in a Geisinger press release.[36]

Before officially launching the program, Geisinger piloted it in Shamokin, Pennsylvania, where more than 20 percent of residents live below the poverty line. Even more striking is that 12 percent of Shamokin residents over the age of 20 have diabetes, and one in three residents is food insecure.[37] Piloting this program at the local level allowed Geisinger to develop and refine the program to meet the unique needs of a high-risk population.

---

36   https://www.prnewswire.com/news-releases/an-rx-for-good-health-geisinger-launches-fresh-food-pharmacy-300360675.html

37   https://www.geisinger.org/about-geisinger/news-and-media/news-releases/2017/03/24/18/42/an-rx-for-good-health

Geisinger's *Plus* Product Solution:
Fresh Food Pharmacy

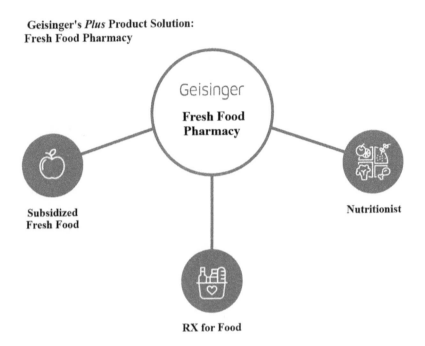

**Subsidized
Fresh Food**

Nutritionist

RX for Food

ADDING VALUE, INCREASING HEALTH

Since its launch, the Fresh Food Pharmacy has proven to be beneficial for both consumers and the health system. The Fresh Food Pharmacy program costs Geisinger nearly $1,000 per participant. The outcomes, however, far outweigh the upfront costs. Geisinger Health evaluates the success of the program by patients' A1C levels, which measure the amount of glucose in the blood. Through research and analysis, Geisinger Health determined that the system saves $8,000 for every one-point decrease in a patient's A1C levels. Within the first year, many of the participants in the program saw a three-point decline in their A1C levels, resulting in savings of nearly $24,000.[38]

---

38   https://www.npr.org/sections/thesalt/2017/05/08/526952657/fresh-food-by-prescription-this-health-care-firm-is-trimming-costs-and-waistline

Given the program's early success, Geisinger is in the process of expanding it to other hospitals across Pennsylvania. Instead of providing reactive healthcare services to patients, Geisinger Health is shifting the paradigm to invest in proactive programs that encourage people to change their behavior. It is no longer enough to anchor patient care to a medication or procedure; the solution surrounding it is necessary to achieve the ultimate goal.

Other organizations are considering solution-oriented programs like Geisinger's that connect the healthcare ecosystem to address common barriers to healthy living but are using partnerships. In early 2018, Blue Cross Blue Shield of Massachusetts invested $18 million in Zipongo, a platform of lifestyle apps to help patients better manage their conditions through behavioral changes.[39] Apps like those on Zipongo could help payers engage with their members at the behavioral level. Zipongo's new FoodScripts app, for example, will add services to the platform that address conditions like diabetes and obesity through personalized and prescriptive nutrition programs. Like the other apps on the platform, FoodScripts is designed to change the consumer's behavior. By collecting personal data, the app's algorithm learns the user's preferences and lifestyle habits and uses this information to suggest shopping lists, recipes and even restaurant recommendations. Much like Geisinger's Fresh Food Pharmacy, FoodScripts enables consumers to proactively address their dietary challenges in effective, sustainable ways. "Our relationship with Zipongo is another solution in our portfolio that ensures that, no matter where someone is, they have the tools they need to lead healthier lives," says Robin Glasco, Chief Innovation Officer at BCBSMA.

---

39 http://www.mobihealthnews.com/content/zipongo-gets-18m-food-prescription-platform

CRAFT SOLUTIONS THAT CONNECT HEALTHCARE PLAYERS

Pharma companies like Germany-based global pharmaceutical company Boehringer Ingelheim (BI) are leveraging partnerships with digital companies to offer value-added services to consumers. BI partnered with Propeller Health, a digital health company involved in chronic obstructive pulmonary disease (COPD) care management. Propeller Health makes a chip that attaches to BI's RESPIMAT® inhaler and tracks a patient's adherence data. That allows the physician to monitor adherence and, if necessary, get in touch with the patient before he or she becomes ill. The data also creates a comprehensive view of the patient's progress so that individuals can view their own condition management. By notifying providers when adherence is low and giving patients a snapshot of their progress, the BI RESPIMAT makes patients aware of their condition before it becomes critical. We will explore the option of digital partnerships more in the "Leveraging Digital to Win" chapter.

As healthcare organizations around the globe continue to be under pressure to deliver value over volume, this type of solution—which allows physicians to remotely identify problems before they become emergencies—will be even more beneficial. "We are now a far stronger enabler of [physicians'] business when their incentives shift to value," says Paul Fonteyne, CEO of BI USA. "We feel much more patient-focused, because we know we developed the medications to avoid costly events that no patients would desire for themselves." By engaging people in this way—giving them ownership of their own data and helping them communicate with physicians—BI proactively manages the challenges facing patients with COPD instead of being entirely reactive.

OFFERING DIGITAL SOLUTIONS AROUND THE WORLD

Other healthcare organizations around the globe are leveraging partnerships with digital health in order to help engage consumers. AIA, the largest publicly-listed, pan-Asian life-insurance group, partners with Vitality, a digital health-engagement tool, to create AIA Vitality, a program that allows consumers to track their health, personalize their wellness programs and earn customized rewards for reaching health goals. The program is a powerful way to connect with consumers beyond the four walls of the office and to integrate the brand into their daily lives. "As you go through the health continuum, everyone will go through good health and ill health at some stage," says Christian Wards, AIA's Director of Group Healthcare. "Consumer behavior and health-seeking behavior are present throughout that whole continuum, and we have to be present, too."

The U.K.'s National Health Service (NHS) partners with digital platforms to increase engagement for chronic illnesses. NHS general practitioners can give consumers a myCOPD management tool, a digitally-enabled engagement tool that, much like BI's RESPIMAT, helps patients track their symptoms and communicate with physicians about condition management and progress.

CONCLUSION: CONNECT ECOSYSTEMS THAT EMBRACE CONSUMERS

The success stories from organizations across the healthcare spectrum demonstrate that, while difficult, taking a solution-oriented mindset is possible. Let's review the key learnings required to make the Second Shift:

Mapping the Journey Provides a Holistic View

When Mount Sinai mapped the journey of TJR patients, the organization was able to better understand where patients were having trouble and where the hospital system and the labor union could intervene. When organizations see obstacles from that vantage point, they can tackle them in the context of the rest of the journey. What is the role of the organization in addressing a pain point, then, given its role in the entire journey?

"Plus Product" Thinking Requires Deliberate Planning

Once an organization has mapped the journey and identified those moments of greatest need, it will need a solution that addresses obstacles to good health. Finding that solution requires thoughtful consideration and planning. What are the barriers that consumer face? Which factors have the greatest impact on those barriers?

Execution Requires a Willingness to Partner

Organizations can build solutions internally, as we saw with Geisinger's Food Pharmacy, but they often lack some of the resources necessary to successfully or efficiently deliver a solution. In that case, partnership offers a great opportunity. To create the TJR solution, Mount Sinai worked with 32BJ in a way that led to beneficial outcomes for both parties. Organizations should consider the number of influencers that surround consumers and evaluate which would be most appropriate and would best complement the expertise of the organization.

Start Small, Then Scale

When Geisinger was piloting its Fresh Food Pharmacy, the organization started with a small, targeted population of low-income consumers with the greatest need. Starting at this level can be key to creating a *Plus Product* solution, as it allows the organization to understand the unique needs of consumers and use that knowledge to design and then evolve effective services and integrated solutions.

The Third Shift

From Population-Centric To Person-Centered

"People define value differently. For someone like myself, who is healthy and busy, high-value care is all about convenience and access. And that's very different from someone who has two different chronic diseases and moves in out and out of homelessness."

–Niyum Gandhi, EVP and Chief Population Health Officer, Mount Sinai Health System

Healthcare organizations struggle to deliver experiences that are relevant to individual needs and preferences. From communications that don't resonate to engagement plans that don't fit the consumer's lifestyle, organizations continue to make healthcare—which is inherently a personal experience—into something that feels impersonal and disconnected. Not only are consumers paying more for their healthcare, they are also increasingly more accustomed to personalized experiences in other areas of their lives—from transportation and entertainment to travel and dining. Healthcare organizations need to deliver the same. "When you have consumers playing an ever-increasing role in brand selection, as well as paying more out of their own pockets for healthcare, especially for drugs, you have to create a value that really resonates with them to win," says Thane Wettig, Vice President of Global Marketing at Eli Lilly and Co. until early 2018. If healthcare organizations can do this, they will be better equipped to engage consumers and improve outcomes.

In the Third Shift, healthcare organizations learn to leverage their understanding of what's relevant to *groups* of consumers in order to tailor experiences that suit the needs and preferences of *individual* consumers. To understand this change better, let's take a close look at how Netflix has mastered the art of delivering personalized experiences and then explore the implications of that for healthcare organizations.

LEARN FROM NETFLIX: WHAT KIND OF PERSONALIZATION MATTERS MOST?

Perhaps the best example of personalization comes from entertainment giant Netflix. The company that revolutionized the movie-watching experience is also redefining what consumers consider personalization. Netflix understands what groups of consumers enjoy, so it can deliver relevant content on a broad level while working tirelessly on personalizing the experience to the individual's needs. Netflix's impressive ability to do this can be attributed to its use of vast viewership data and analytics. Netflix records, tracks and analyzes data regarding the content that users watch, the time users spend selecting a movie and even the number of times people pause or stop playback. As much value as consumers gain from the Netflix service, Netflix gains just as much value in exchange. The most obvious application of that data is the personalized movie recommendations that appear on a user's home screen, but the incorporation of the data into the experience goes far beyond that. After six years of data collection, Netflix executed its most well-known use of data—the development of original content. The hit series *Orange Is the New Black* resulted from viewer insights regarding the storylines that consumers enjoy in the shows they watch, what keeps them hooked and the types of characters they enjoy watching.[40] Netflix has created other shows in which every stage of production was rooted in insights, right down to the trailers that viewers are shown.[41]

As Netflix accumulates more data, it explores new ways to personalize experiences. For instance, Netflix is considering expanding the use of artificial intelligence to help create personalized movie trailers based on viewer preferences.[42] Some viewers are more likely to watch a film with a romantic storyline, so their trailer might highlight love scenes. Others may select content based on a favorite actor, so those trailers will reflect that. Netflix is making what used to be a generic experience—watching a standard trailer—and tailoring it to the individual. It's part of the reason Netflix fans are so loyal.

Spotify and Delta have also committed to creating personalized experiences. Spotify curates a "Discover Weekly" playlist based on a

---

40   https://hbr.org/2018/01/data-can-enhance-creative-projects-just-look-at-netflix

41   https://www.nytimes.com/2013/02/25/business/media/for-house-of-cards-using-big-data-to-guarantee-its-popularity.html

42   https://www.theregister.co.uk/2017/12/06/personalised_netflix_trailers_could_be_coming_to_you_soon/

user's listening history, as well as on the streaming habits of users with similar taste. The playlist introduces users to new music, encouraging curiosity and increasing the value of a Spotify membership. Delta has personalized the in-flight experience by arming flight attendants with details about each flyer, such as their Delta status or past experiences. With this information, flight attendants can personally thank specific customers for their corporate partnership or apologize for an inconvenience that the customer may have previously reported. Companies like those have harnessed extensive data to better understand consumer preferences and behavioral patterns and are incorporating that knowledge into unexpected, but inspired, personalized experiences.

THE CHALLENGE FOR HEALTHCARE: SEEING PAST POPULATION-BASED MYOPIA

Like Netflix and Spotify, healthcare organizations have access to enormous amounts of data that hold the potential to create personalized experiences across the non-clinical aspects of care, such as appointment scheduling, billing or treatment-plan adherence. Despite having a wealth of data, the healthcare industry has yet to unleash its potential. When we surveyed healthcare leaders about personalized experiences, more than half reported that they fail to use data to customize communication channels and content. Even the most basic interactions that consumers have with an organization are generic when they could be customized. This lack of tailoring impacts the experience and also hurts engagement. "You think about all the other things that go on," says Sheri Dodd, Vice President and General Manager of Medtronic Care Management Services, a service business within Medtronic, plc, a medical device company, "like making sure questions are relevant to the patient's condition, reading and comprehension skills. Relatability matters in patient engagement. Don't call a female 'he' or ask patients to identify with a scenario that doesn't look anything like the one they are in. Patients have to see a value in the engagement, and personalization matters." A truly personalized healthcare experience not only strengthens the organization's relationship with consumers but also improves impact and engagement.

To create individualized solutions, healthcare organizations need to better understand and anticipate the consumer's needs, wants and motivations and use that understanding to create personalized experiences. Our discussions with healthcare leaders revealed that gaining a more nuanced understanding of consumers requires two stages: First, healthcare organizations can use insights from groups of similar consumers (sometimes called personas) to create products, services, experiences and communications. Second, using insights from the selected personas, organizations can build on that foundation and incorporate an individual's data to personalize the product or service.

To reiterate, insights from personas determine the direction for product, service and experience design. Individual data takes the process a step further to customize the experience to an individual's needs. One way to create personas is through a quantitatively derived segmentation analysis, which divides large heterogeneous groups of people into smaller groups of like-minded consumers according to preferences, needs, wants, attitudes and behaviors. A segmentation analysis gives organizations a better understanding of their consumers and will help inform the relevant product, service, experience and content strategies to execute. From there, organizations can use real-time data collection and sophisticated AI analysis to activate their offerings at the individual level. "The ability to collect data is colliding with the need to bring more value to the healthcare system," says Frank Cunningham, Vice President, Managed Healthcare Services,

Eli Lilly and Company. "There is a huge opportunity to understand more about patients and what is happening in their lives and use that understanding to benefit the patient through better medicines and services."

Together, these two steps can help turn good healthcare into high-quality, personalized and relevant healthcare.

Getting to Person-Centered:

1   *Use insights from groups of similar consumers (sometimes called personas) to create products, services, experiences and communications*

2   *Use insights from the selected personas to build on this foundation and incorporate individual data to personalize the product or service*

HOW TO MAKE THE SHIFT: USE INSIGHTS TO INFORM PRODUCTS AND SERVICES

One path to increasing personalization is leveraging consumer insights that go well beyond a demographic understanding. As we have learned, engaging consumers in their health requires a behavioral change that demographics alone can't drive. Instead of looking at the market as a heterogeneous group of people, a segmentation analysis identifies personas that represent groups of people with common characteristics. Once an organization understands the various groups within a population, it can set priorities and develop new ideas for how best to win.

LEARN FROM NOVANT HEALTH: NEW PERSONAS REVEAL BETTER PROSPECTS

In 2013, Novant Health, a North Carolina-based hospital system, announced a strategic plan to formally unify all programs, services and facilities under a single operating unit. After several mergers, acquisitions and partnerships, the four-state integrated health system expanded to include 13 hospitals, 500 outpatient clinics, 1,300 physicians, nine million customers and $4 billion in revenue. The challenge was to unify the system, which previously operated under 350 different brand names, and to gain relevance. To do this well, Novant Health had to gain a deeper understanding of the groups within the populations so it could design mechanisms to engage consumers in relevant ways. "We had to agree that the right way forward was to compare ourselves to iconic brands outside of healthcare—not to aspire to be them but, rather, to be inspired by them—and connecting with individual consumers in ways that meet their unique needs," said David Duvall, Senior Vice President, Chief Marketing and Communications.

Part of getting to a single, unified system involved creating services that resonate with Novant Health's different populations of consumers. To do that, Duvall's team conducted rigorous research to derive a segmentation solution that was both strategic and achievable. The research examined thousands of patients, potential patients and caregivers on multiple levels, from price sensitivity and smartphone usage to time spent on the internet and social media engagement. The research uncovered six key personas:

1. **Eager and Engaged Stewards**...actively involved with healthcare, with many who are caretakers for both children and parents

2. **Savvy and Connected Patients**...enjoy taking care of their health and are looking to maintain and increase their involvement in healthcare
3. **Healthy and Unconcerned Individuals**...want as few interactions as possible and engage with healthcare providers only when necessary
4. **Cost-Conscious Guidance Seekers**...frugal but willing to pay for access to services they value
5. **Responsible and Resolute Boomers**...prefer one-on-one care interactions with providers and are averse to alternative and digital care
6. **Uninterested and Unengaged Individuals**...attribute minimal value to an improved care experience

Novant Health: Consumer Segmentation

Eager & Engaged Stewards	Savvy & Connected	Healthy & Unconcerned
18%	29%	24%
SEGMENT SIZE	SEGMENT SIZE	SEGMENT SIZE
Cost Conscious Guidance Seekers	Responsible & Resolute Boomers	Uninterested & Unengaged
6%	14%	8%
SEGMENT SIZE	SEGMENT SIZE	SEGMENT SIZE

Novant Health identified the first two segments as a primary focus, with the goal of increasing their engagement and loyalty while building familiarity and consideration with the other four segments. With an increased understanding of those discrete segments, cross-functional teams at Novant Health joined forces to design products and services to meet the needs of each group.

Segmentation enabled the system to identify common needs that resonate most with target segments. Because Novant Health needs to serve all consumers, however, the organization identified the top needs in all segments, such as cost clarity, access and digital integration. Those insights led to the development of services such as *Your Healthcare Costs*, an online feature that helps consumers understand complex healthcare finance information. Insights from the segmentation also led to the development of *Care Connections*, a 24-hour virtual care hub with services such as nurse triage, online scheduling, wellness coaching, discharge follow-ups, medication management and psychosocial consults. The care-navigation feature is perfectly designed for the Eager and Engaged Stewards, who seek providers that can help them lead healthier lives, by adding digital services to their healthcare interactions. Finally, the insights catalyzed the hospital system's digital transformation, leading to the development of products such as *HoldMyPlace* for urgent-care reservations, *Open Schedule* for viewing physician availability and online scheduling through *MyChart*. Those services are particularly relevant to consumers within the Savvy and Connected segment, who prize seamless care and digital communications and services.

In addition to providing direction on service and to offering design, Novant Health's segmentation helped illuminate the communication preferences of each of the six segments. That included insight into what should be said, how it should be said and through what platform it should be communicated. Preferences included insight into a consumer's skepticism or trust toward the healthcare industry, whether to use a formal or informal tone of voice and even how thorough or concise the communications should be. That level of insight allowed Novant Health to tailor messaging to consumers both inside and outside the clinic and led to the development of a set of communication guidelines for system employees. That level of individual understanding doesn't just make the experience more personal, it also makes it more human. Most interactions with healthcare organizations are not by choice. They are often situations of uncertainty and stress; so honoring communicating preferences is a small, yet meaningful, step toward putting consumers at ease.

Mine People's Data for More Relevance

Creating services and offerings based on insights from different segments, as highlighted in the Novant Health example, ultimately allows for more relevant engagement with consumers. Organizations don't have to stop there, though. They can take it a step further and create personalized experiences using the data collected on individual consumers. Spotify, for example, uses listener data to curate playlists for certain moods or activities, which leads to relevancy. To get *more* personalized, Spotify takes individual streaming data to make personalized Discovery playlists for an individual. As outside companies like Spotify create new expectations for personalized experiences, being able to turn consumer data into relevant healthcare experiences will be a key basis for competition. "If you were to serve up relevant information to make a sale, it would be creepy," says Rob Odom, Vice President of Marketing and Brand Management at UCSF. "But when you use it to serve up a better experience, you're providing real value to the patient." The challenge in healthcare is capturing and the identifying the right data to drive more personal offerings.

Fortunately, consumers are willing to share their data with healthcare organizations, particularly if the consumer gets something out of it. Providers, especially, have an opportunity, because consumers trust their information being with providers more than with health plans or employers. Surveys show that a patient's willingness to share data is higher when it comes to information from passive monitoring devices.[43] More than a quarter of internet users, across 17 countries, strongly agree that they are willing to share their personal data in exchange for benefits or rewards or personalized service.[44] In a study conducted by Accenture, about 90 percent of consumers are open to sharing wearable or app data with a doctor; 87 percent, with a nurse. Today, about 40 percent of health app users have already done so.[45] That data can be key to engagement, because it allows both the system at large and physicians on an individual basis to get a more up-to-date picture of the patient. "I could try to collect as much data as possible, but if a patient doesn't provide their side of the data or story, like their biometric measurements or they don't report their symptoms, I only have half the story," says Medtronic's Dodd. "Data gets you insights. Insights inform opportunities to impact outcomes. So, how do I get patients to engage, not just one time, and not just three times, but for six months? That's tough to do."

The task for healthcare organizations is determining what mechanism they can use to gather that data and how to reward consumers who share. Some organizations have successfully built data-collecting strategies in-house, and others have partnered with external players who have greater access to patients across the journey. Using partners for gathering patient data is particularly common in the pharmaceutical industry, where there are tight regulations around interacting directly

43   https://med.stanford.edu/content/dam/sm/sm-news/documents/
      StanfordMedicineHealthTrendsWhitePaper2017.pdf

44   https://www.gfk.com/fileadmin/user_upload/country_one_pager/NL/images/
      Global-GfK_onderzoek_-_delen_van_persoonlijke_data.pdf

45   https://www.accenture.com/_acnmedia/PDF-8/Accenture-Patients-Want-A-
      Heavy-Dose-of-Digital-Infographic-v2.pdf

with patients. For example, pharma company Bayer has partnered with Chinese retail giant Alibaba to get access to the company's wealth of consumer data. That partnership allows Bayer to better understand the behaviors and preferences of consumers in China.

Delivering on Your Data Promises: Use Data for Good

To overcome the challenge of getting a reluctant public to share data, we recommend that our clients develop what we call a Consumer Data Value Exchange (CDVE): a mechanism for determining what consumers will receive in return for sharing personal data. Developing an effective CDVE requires a few key steps: The organization theorizes how data can add value for both the consumer *and* the business, what touchpoints in the journey are appropriate for data collection and what the process (e.g. opt-in) for data collection will look like. Then, the organization codifies it in a specific, motivating value-exchange proposition that will resonate with consumers. Finally, the organization deploys the value exchange proposition.

Consumer Data Value Exchange (CDVE) Model

ORGANIZATION VALUE
How does data create value for the organization?

CONSUMER VALUE
How does data create value for the consumer?

DATA REQUIREMENTS
What data is required to create value for the organization and the consumers?

OPT-IN CHOICES
How can the organization collect the necessary data?

What touchpoints   What process   What experience

The CDVE strategy is common in industries outside of healthcare. For example, Nike+ Run Club enables users to have real-time GPS tracking details of their runs, combined with a database of past runs and customized coaching plans. The application also provides social features, which incentivize consumers to share location and running data with Nike in return for the personalized and motivational experience. Consumer data from Nike+ Run Club has allowed Nike to amass proprietary data that the company consistently leverages to create more personalized digital and physical customer relationships, as well as to inform the development of new footwear and apparel. In the insurance industry, Progressive's Snapshot app automatically monitors and measures drivers' data—such as time of day, mileage and hard braking—and offer discounts on premiums for safe driving. At the end of each trip, through the app, users are shown personalized information about their trip, a rating, a map of their drive and personalized tips to help them improve their score. Through Snapshot, Progressive has gathered and analyzed valuable driving data that not only encourages safe driving but also provides an accurate and objective claims process based on real driving data.

There are some examples of compelling CDVEs in healthcare, too. PatientsLikeMe is a network that allows patients living with chronic conditions to track and share their experiences and improve outcomes. The company also works with major pharmaceutical companies, including Merck and AstraZeneca, to help them understand what it's like to live with a disease and to bring the patient voice into the development and delivery processes. "Over the years, we have seen consumer empowerment become more important. Organizations need to not only learn about what patients are actually experiencing but also embed that into their strategy and delivery of care," says Michael Evers, Executive Vice President Technology, Marketing, and Operations until May 2018. PatientsLikeMe is designed to be a community that benefits others, and all users can access others' reviews and experiences to gain a better understanding of their own illnesses and options. PatientsLikeMe aggregates data submitted by patients and sells it to companies creating new drugs, devices, equipment, insurance plans and medical services. By selling data, PatientsLikeMe helps companies accelerate the development of new solutions for patients. The organization's CDVE, called "Data for Good," was the foundation of PatientsLikeMe's business model, until it became part of iCarbonX in 2018. As the company explains, "Your data has a heartbeat that gives life to medical research. Donate your data for you, for others, for good."

Insurance companies have more trouble gathering consumer data than others, because consumers trust insurance companies less. American insurer Aetna has overcome this challenge through a partnership with Apple Watch. The Apple Watch program gives members the device for free and integrates the data with Aetna's already existing data. By offering members the free device, Aetna incentivizes consumers to exercise more and to live healthier lifestyles. In return, the data allows Aetna to engage consumers at a personal level and target them with content that is relevant.

LEARN FROM GEISINGER HEALTH: DIGITAL BREADCRUMBS YIELD SMARTER SERVICE

Some organizations can build data collection platforms on their own. Geisinger Health implemented a new IT system in 2015 that integrates big data into its existing analytics systems. The system consolidates data from clinical departments, health and wellness apps and patient satisfaction surveys. "Looking at patients solely through the lens of an EHR yields an incomplete picture; patients visit clinics outside of the health system's reach and, in fact, spend the vast majority of their time outside of healthcare systems altogether," writes systems executives Alistair R. Erskine, M.D., Bipin Karunakaran, M.D., Jonathan R. Slotkin, M.D. and David T. Feinberg, M.D. in a 2015 *Harvard Business Review* article.[46] "They leave digital breadcrumbs everywhere they interact, from the grocery store and its loyalty program to the smartphone and its apps." With the patient's permission, Geisinger's system also collects data from smartphones, grocery reward cards and other health and wellness-related programs.

In addition to integrating data from daily activities, the system can perform analytics on free-text imaging reports to identify patients with critically large abdominal aortic aneurysms who didn't have follow-up appointments and to identify other at-risk patients. By integrating this data, the system can provide a more holistic view of the patient and flag potential health risks before they become emergencies. In 2016, Geisinger enhanced the data-collection strategy and launched a new program that collects real-time patient data from the waiting room before the physician even sees the patient. Patients with chronic conditions—such as heart disease, asthma and arthritis—are handed a tablet in the waiting room to answer questions. The information automatically enters Geisinger's system before the appointment and alerts the care team to any needed blood work or other tests.

Push AI Beyond Clinical Applications

As the amount of healthcare data grows, its value for personalized experiences will continue to increase. One way that organizations can get value out of this data is through artificial intelligence. Unlike other, more static forms of data collection, AI adds automatic experience improvement by responding to real-time feedback. The more data the consumer gives, the smarter the algorithm becomes—just as the more

---

46   https://hbr.org/2016/12/how-geisinger-health-system-uses-big-data-to-save-lives

you watch Netflix, the better the personalized recommendations. Before AI organizations could measure a consumer's specific actions, they had to make assumptions based on associations with demographics. As discovered over time, demographics don't tell us much. "There's a lot you can do with certain information–age, set of symptoms, attitudes—but that information can take you only so far. Now you can take that info and fold in actual behavior. Then you can create real personalization," says Susan Etlinger, an analyst with Prophet's Altimeter.

For AI to work, three factors need to be in place: First, the organization needs enough data for the algorithm to become smarter. Second, the computing power must be cost-effective for the system and not require a complete overhaul. Third, the algorithm must be sophisticated enough to adapt to feedback and provide real-time information to improve offerings and experiences.

The most common uses of AI in healthcare are clinical: Predicative diagnostics, imaging diagnostics and conversational AI. While AI in healthcare is typically discussed regarding its application to clinical care, AI also holds potential for value in designing personalized nonclinical experiences. In fact, AI's predictive capabilities are being tested in non-clinical settings across some of America's leading hospital systems. At Beth Israel Deaconess Medical Center in Boston, technologists are exploring a machine-learning model to predict which patients are most likely to miss an appointment. Being able to identify those patients would allow the hospital to intervene ahead of time.[47]

---

47   http://www.modernhealthcare.com/indepth/artificial-intelligence-in-healthcare-makes-slow-impact/

Targeting New Customers

After Novant Health completed its segmentation, Duvall knew the system needed to take personalization further. That next step involved partnering with a digital-marketing firm to use advanced computing to improve the consumer experience. Novant Health's partner mined consumer search history; if a consumer previously searched knee replacement surgeries, for example, the digital-marketing firm would push relevant content regarding Novant Health's service offerings and physicians. The system also geotargets potential consumers moving into Novant Health's service areas, using the U.S. Postal Service's National Change of Address (NCOA) database and freal-estate platforms like Zillow, and reaches out to people moving into the Charlotte area. "With all the competitive activity happening in Charlotte, we can win disproportionately by getting to consumers faster. We shifted from traditional advertising and promotions to tailored content that gets [people] to lean in and respond to our calls to action," Duvall says.

This partnership has not only allowed Novant Health to leverage new types of data for consumer acquisition but also helps to integrate insights from the segmentation into Epic, the medical-records software. Using the information on new customers, Novant Health's partner can integrate communication tips into Epic so the staff knows how to interact with those newcomers upon the first interaction. Better yet, that initiative, which would have taken years for an in-house team to complete, was rolled out in months. "We need to create a more authentic and more relevant brand experience in the consumer's healthcare journey, and we can't do that alone," Duvall says.

CONCLUSION: ENGAGE EACH PERSON, NOT THE WHOLE POPULATION

As engagement becomes critical in the healthcare space, organizations must deliver personalized experiences. Reaching beyond broad populations to individuals requires a toolbox of approaches. Let's review them:

Segmentation Takes You Far

As we saw with Novant Health, conducting a market segmentation gives organizations a better understanding of who their consumers are and how the organization can design services for those groups of people. Market segmentation can provide clarity on what the greatest needs are and help prioritize certain groups of people. Organizations can ask: What are the needs and preferences of groups in the market? Which needs are greatest, and how can we build relevant services or enhance the already existent ones to meet those needs?

Individual Data Takes You Further

Market segmentation will help guide the development of services for personas, but individual data will allow an organization to deliver those services in a manner tailored to individual needs. Organizations will have to make several considerations and develop a strategy for collecting that data. Which touchpoints present opportunities for data collection? What value does the organization promise to consumers who offer their data? As we saw with PatientsLikeMe and Novant Health, collecting and integrating the data sometimes requires partnership.

The Fourth Shift

From Incremental Improvements To Pervasive Innovation

"Innovation should not just be siloed within a function. It needs to run through the veins of the organization."
—Robin Glasco, Chief Innovation Officer,
Blue Cross Blue Shield of Massachusetts

I t's no secret that the healthcare industry is going through an enormous amount of change, including the transformation of reimbursement models, rising costs and rapidly evolving consumer expectations. The healthcare industry is anything but stagnant. But instead of becoming more open, executives across the board agree that, when it comes to consumer experience and engagement innovation, the industry is risk-averse. That cautiousness continues to widen the gap between consumer expectations and what healthcare organizations can deliver. And it dramatically impacts their ability to influence consumer behavior outside the clinic.

To adapt to the changes that consumers demand, healthcare organizations need to make the Fourth Shift, which involves moving from incremental improvements to relentless and pervasive innovation. This shift explores how organizations can spark innovation and maintain it over time, making innovation an integral part of the way in which the organization runs its business and serves consumers. Experience and engagement innovation must become a responsibility that permeates the entire organization. Before we dive into what that means for healthcare, let's look at how cosmetic retailer Sephora used pervasive innovation to save its business when traditional retail sales started to migrate to digital. It's an apt analogy for healthcare, which is also operating in a fast-changing environment.

LEARN FROM SEPHORA: SHAKE UP YOUR INNOVATION MACHINE

From augmented-reality eyebrows to Instagram-inspired shopping experiences, Sephora has created engaging and relevant experiences and offerings that transcend both the digital and physical worlds. Sephora was born of an innovative spirit, as it transformed the cosmetic industry from stale department stores to a candy store-like experiences that inspire discovery, confidence and fun. While the Sephora model was successful for many years, the company had yet to face its biggest challenge—digital retail. Consumers were deserting brick-and-mortar stores, shaking the retail industry and threatening to disrupt Sephora's model, which was anchored on consumers experimenting with the various products in its stores. If Sephora were to stay relevant, it would need to reimagine the way consumers shopped for cosmetics. To do that, Sephora put innovation into an exciting environment, hired people with innovative minds, studied the needs of consumers and developed processes for quick test-and-learns. True to its pioneering roots, Sephora used those strategies to revamp innovation efforts and once again transformed the cosmetic shopping experience.

To spark bold new thinking, Sephora took innovation out of its corporate offices in San Francisco and placed it in a new home where innovators could explore and play with new concepts. In 2015, The Innovation Lab was born in a converted warehouse near San Francisco's Mission Bay district. The space, which was previously used to design and assess in-store display models, became a place to develop and test innovative experiences for mobile, web and brick-and-mortar platforms. The Innovation Lab team, comprised of creative and digitally minded people, convenes in the space twice a week and holds testing sessions with store employees to develop new and innovative concepts and experiences. The Innovation Lab allows Sephora to test new concepts in a small, controlled space. And after testing and learning in the lab, Sephora tests the experience concepts in select stores, making any necessary adjustments before scaling the concepts across regions. Instead of investing in a full overhaul of systems, the innovation team can evaluate concepts in beta, gather feedback and then observe results in market.

Sephora's Innovation Lab explores the intersection of the in-store and digital experiences to create a singular, cohesive consumer strategy. This is arguably its strongest aspect of innovation. Since moving to digital platforms, Sephora has not lost the magic of the in-store experience—because both platforms are equally important. The collaborative nature of shopping at Sephora comes to life digitally through Sephora's Beauty Board, a Pinterest-like platform where consumers can view and shop the looks of other people as Sephora does with Virtual Artist, an augmented-reality feature on the app that lets women try on products. Digital innovation does not compromise the in-store experience; rather, digital innovation enhances the in-store experience and connects it to other platforms. "So much of what we're doing is focused on technology and how it leads to the in-store experience or how a client will use her own phone in our stores," says Bridget Dolan, Vice President of the Innovation Lab, in an interview with *Fast Company.*[48] "We created this space for that reason. It's also meant to be a place where we can get outside of our four walls and think about big ideas and test those ideas, meet vendors, test their technologies."

At Sephora, innovation is never done for innovation's sake. The organization instead uses innovation to get to the crux of the company's role as partner in beauty—and to do it better than before. Innovation isn't just about new devices, programs or offerings. It is also about discovering new ways of getting things done. Innovation can come in the form of business-model transformation or process enhancements that allow organizations to deliver better products, services and experiences, resulting in greater impact and relevance. Establishing innovation as part of an organization's DNA is critical to Sephora and is crucial to healthcare's successful transformation to consumer centricity.

THE CHALLENGE FOR HEALTHCARE: MAKE FRESH THINKING LESS FRIGHTENING

Much like Sephora, healthcare organizations must convert a business that has historically engaged consumers in person to one that

---

48   https://www.fastcompany.com/3043166/first-look-inside-sephoras-new-innovation-lab

is relevant on a variety of platforms. Compared to other consumer services, healthcare is far behind. One reason is that organizations tend to approach experience and engagement innovation in the same way they tackle clinical breakthroughs. Clinical innovation demands incredible precision and caution and requires multiple rounds of testing and analysis until the final product has been perfected and approved by appropriate governing bodies. While long processes are warranted in clinical research, they stifle healthcare experience and engagement innovation, which need not be scrutinized in the same way. That upfront investment and time also discourage experimentation with experience design. "Health organizations have bad innovation memory because of the upfront effort and organizational change it requires," says Sterling Lanier, CEO of Tonic Health, a leading electronic patient data-collection company among large health systems. "When things go awry, the lesson is not that the idea was faulty or that the execution was flawed. The lesson is that innovation is faulty." That creates a culture in which employees don't feel free to take chances. That risk aversion isn't surprising, given the amount of regulation within the healthcare industry. Organizations have good reason to be risk-averse, as they seek to avoid litigation, HIPAA violations and privacy breaches.

Given the extensive procedural barriers that organizations must overcome, unsuccessful innovation breeds a culture of cynicism, skepticism and complacency. That is particularly true within pharma companies trying to explore digital assets, says Louis Zollo, former Director of Global Portfolio Management at Teva Pharmaceuticals until 2018. "There are a tremendous number of dead apps and ineffective online programs that don't actually create any value," he says. "People don't use them, and they only take up space." This negative feedback loop further discourages innovation.

Because healthcare organizations hesitate to fully embrace and invest in experience and engagement innovation, they can lack the structure and talent necessary to accelerate new ideas. Creative thinkers are key to driving innovation, as they can translate an understanding of consumers into solutions that improve the entire consumer experience. If organizations lack innovative mindsets, there is no mechanism for solving consumer needs in a new way; as a result, the organization won't meet the rising expectations of consumers. "On both the competitive side and the consumer expectation side, we are seeing that the definition of consumer centricity keeps getting elevated. We have to continue to innovate and push ourselves to maintain both consumer relevance and a competitive edge," says IU Health CEO Dennis Murphy.

SOLVING HEALTHCARE'S IDEA SHORTAGE

If healthcare organizations want to keep up with the competition and improve engagement, they need to radically transform innovation practices that run through the organization. That requires more efficient and agile approaches and mindsets. "Of course, you have to respect the regulations; but you must be bold in your decisions. Commit to reaching out to consumers, investing in experimentation, taking some chances," says Reynick Martinez, former Chief Marketing and Communications Officer at Presence Health. Organizations must foster a stronger culture in which experimentation is embraced, employees are encouraged and rewarded for new ideas and appropriate support structures are in place to bring these efforts to life. Our research revealed that, depending on the resources and structure of an organization, healthcare organizations can spark innovation in a few different ways:

- Mirror the strategy of startups and apply the Minimal Viable Product (MVP) concept to innovation.
- Form an internal startup or incubator program to unite the most innovative minds in the company for brainstorming and designing new ideas.
- Outsource innovation to external organizations.

How to Spark Healthcare Innovation:

1	2	3
Mirror the strategy of startups and apply the Minimal Viable Product (MVP) concept to innovation	Form an internal startup or incubator program to unite the most innovative minds in the company for brainstorming and designing new ideas	Outsource innovation to external organizations

APPLYING THE MVP APPROACH

As consumer expectations rise, organizations must move quickly to meet those needs. Startups do this very well; and while there are many startup techniques that healthcare organizations cannot adopt due to the regulatory environment, one technique they *can* use is the minimal viable product (MVP) approach. MVP is a trial-and-error approach, by which an organization releases an idea as version 1.0 and then continues to make updates and improvements until the product becomes final. The MVP approach accelerates the innovation process by securing the minimum amount of resources required to prove impact and gather evangelists, who will then help improve and expand the product. Dr. Erskine says Geisinger Health System uses this approach for its efforts: "We support innovation in the form of rapid prototyping, meaning three months to show minimum viable product within a production system with a limited number of providers, a limited number of patients and a limited amount of time to demonstrate adoption and impact."

In traditional stage-gate innovation processes, the upfront investment of time and finances can cause organizational burnout and fatigue. The MVP approach helps avoid that issue by pursuing innovation in a step-by-step process rather than a complete overhaul. Another benefit of the step-by-step process is that it allows for modifications and improvements as the organization receives feedback on the first version. "We want to focus on what we call 'low-resolution' solutions before we spend millions of dollars on the 'high-resolution' solution. Let's put our focus into building the right thing for consumers rather than wasting time on perfection," says Robin Glasco, Chief Innovation Officer at Blue Cross Blue Shield of Massachusetts.

LEARN FROM ADVOCATE HEALTH CARE: SAME-DAY MAMMOGRAMS IGNITE BIGGER CHANGES

One of the Midwest's largest health systems, Advocate Health Care (Advocate Aurora Health as of April 2018) used an MVP approach to begin its journey to same-day appointment scheduling. As Advocate worked to deepen its relationship with consumers, the organization found that convenience and access were two areas where the system could improve. The ideal solution would be online, same-day self-scheduling so that consumers could have more freedom to decide when they receive healthcare. Advocate understood that overhauling its entire scheduling system would be a painful, and possibly unsuccessful, effort. Such an overhaul would require massive changes at the core hospital systems and also in specialty clinics. Structurally, this would be a big ask of the system's IT department and physicians, *and* it would require a massive cultural change. So Advocate started small, leveraging an MVP approach and mindset.

The process began with a project called "Call Today, Be Seen Today," which allowed same-day scheduling for mammograms. The organization realized that consumers did not just want educational materials about breast cancer; they also wanted greater access to care. If Advocate could expand access, Advocate would also expand business. "We realized this consumerism goes far beyond an advertising campaign," says Advocate's Chief Marketing and Digital Officer, Kelly Jo Golson. "We needed operations to help us grow our efforts and better serve our patients." By focusing on mammography, Advocate could control the number of changes necessary to implement the new program, quickly measure results and make real-time updates before investing in an entire restructuring. The single focus also allowed the program to gain advocates who could speak about its impact and how best to roll it out. Advocate experienced double-digit growth after "Call Today, Be Seen Today" was activated, as the new program doubled the number of same-day appointments made and tripled the number of new appointments made. More importantly, the program increased engagement in the breast cancer-awareness campaign, which both benefits consumers' long-term health and drives mammogram business to the system.

After the success of "Call Today, Be Seen Today," Advocate rolled out the 2.0 version of the initiative, which included same-day results. "Call Today, Be Seen Today, Get Results Today" addressed the pain point of delayed results that we found in our joint Patient Experience study with GE Healthcare Partners. "We needed to understand consumer expectations and the natural anxiety that you have going into a mammogram. You sit there biting your nails for two, three, four days until you get that confirmation that all's okay," says Golson. The preliminary roll-out of "Call Today, Be Seen Today" allowed Advocate to evaluate other consumer needs and use the first release as the foundation. The success of both programs gave Advocate the confidence to move forward with offerings in other departments and work its way towards online scheduling across the system.

An organizational mindset shift that focuses on *purpose over process* is important to making the MVP approach work. Starting with a strong innovation purpose, such as helping more women get tested earlier for breast cancer, pushed the team to focus on getting to the right answer to solve the challenge sooner. Beginning with process, on the other hand, tends to lead to a reasoning of why the idea will *not* work. Processes should be informed by asking how the organization can deliver the best outcome for consumers. This purpose-first, process-second mindset better enables employees to deliver on consumer centricity rather than being bogged down by unnecessary systems that hinder innovation. We will talk more about the power of purpose over process in "Creating a Consumer-Centric Culture."

The MVP Approach in Action: Advocate Aurora Health

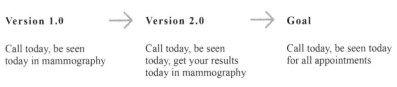

Version 1.0	→	Version 2.0	→	Goal
Call today, be seen today in mammography		Call today, be seen today, get your results today in mammography		Call today, be seen today for all appointments

AdvocateAuroraHealth

CREATE AN INTERNAL STARTUP

One way to overcome the risk aversion that plagues healthcare is to separate innovation efforts from the core business, much as Sephora did with its Innovation Lab. Creating a separate environment for innovation can protect new ideas from the bureaucracy that inhibits progress.

Throughout our discussions with healthcare leaders, we learned that the challenge of risk aversion is particularly acute in the pharmaceutical industry. The regulatory nature of pharma not only stifles experience innovation but also fails to attract entrepreneurial minds with risk-taking attitudes. To solve that, some pharma companies are creating a separate, internal function with a completely different culture that inspires innovative thinking. German pharmaceutical company Boehringer Ingelheim, for example, formed a digital innovation lab called BI X. The team operates like a startup, working closely with all three business units of the company: human pharma, animal health and biopharmaceuticals. BI X is a space for collaboration between and among specialists in data science, agile software development and user-experience design. "Being a separate legal entity from the parent house, BI X combines the freedom of a startup with the power of one of the world's leading pharma companies," the company says in its announcement.[49]

In addition to being physically separate from the parent pharmaceutical company, the digital innovation lab has its own recruitment process to attract innovative talent. "Our ambition is to save and improve lives by developing smarter healthcare solutions. To do so, we need to be digital pioneers. Adventurers who push the boundaries of what is possible and rise to every challenge," says the website. By operating internally, BI still benefits from the proprietary innovation that comes out of the lab. Speaking at a recent industry conference, Larry Brooks, Director of Digital Health at Boehringer Ingelheim, described BI X as marrying the agility of a startup with the financial advantages of the BI parent company. "I think the spirit of it is, essentially, it takes the value of a startup and a pharma company into one unique entity…An in-house development shop that puts programs forward in a set of sprints will enable people within BI to

---

49   https://www.boehringer-ingelheim.com/press-release/boehringer-ingelheim-builds-digital-lab-bi-x

see it and touch it and experience it—and, hopefully, that'll gather the right momentum within the organization to carry things forward and still be enabled by a lot of external groups," he says in an interview with *Mobihealthnews*.[50] The BI X Lab launched in summer of 2017, and the organization invested 10 million euros in the lab within the first year. Other healthcare companies are also using separate innovation labs, such as Johnson & Johnson's Innovation Center, Anthem's Innovation Studio and Mayo Clinic's Center for Innovation. Those organizations are all exploring innovation possibilities in a new environment, inspiring a more agile way of approaching experience and engagement.

LOOK OUTSIDE FOR INSPIRATION

Given the constraints that innovation faces in the healthcare industry, many organizations look to outside industries for guidance and inspiration. Organizations do this in various ways, such as investing in digital health companies, acquiring innovative entities or even creating external councils of innovative thought leaders.

Life sciences companies commonly turn to digital health companies for new thinking, and their approach can provide a good example for the rest of the category. CBInsights analyzed pharma investments and acquisitions in digital-health startups and discovered 13 out of the top 20 pharma companies have a dedicated venture arm, because it allows the company to access new ideas that could transform its businesses. "We are seeding ideas that could grow into something very different from the businesses that we would normally get into," says Susan Ringdal, Hikma's Vice President of Corporate Strategy and Investor Relations. "Some might be things that we could

---

50   http://www.mobihealthnews.com/content/health-20-pharma-companies-talk-partnerships-digital-opportunities-and-still-far-promise

benefit from over time and that may help us evolve into a totally different company." Pharma companies, more so than providers and payers, are cash- and margin-rich, allowing them to invest in innovation that benefits their organizations.

Some pharma companies, however, invest beyond the venture arm and combine the expertise of their people with the innovative thinking of others. One example of that type of external outsourcing comes from Bayer. The German pharmaceutical organization formed LifeScience iHUB, a special facility that orchestrates collaborations between tech companies and Bayer. The team focuses on innovation that spans pharmaceutical, consumer health and agricultural science. The iHUB is located at Singularity University, at NASA Research Park in the heart of Silicon Valley. There, Bayer iHUB can learn about and gain access to the world's most significant digital innovations and test the ways in which those innovations can be incorporated into Bayer's core business. "We're still a company that, by and large, depends on selling its drugs," says Dirk Schapeler, Vice President of Innovation in the United States, in an interview with *MedCityNews*.[51] "But, we are looking a lot toward, 'How can we provide healthcare to patients?'—not only through pills but also through other means."

Employees at Bayer's iHUB generate an idea or concept internally and then partner with leaders at Bayer Pharmaceuticals and Consumer Health who have an unmet need to develop a business case. The leaders at Bayer are tasked with garnering strategic support and sufficient resources; then, the LifeScience iHUB identifies external innovation partners to lead the development the solution. "We see ourselves as the link between technology startups and Bayer. We bring these two worlds together to support Bayer's LifeScience

---

business with new digital solutions," Schapeler says.[52] The iHUB demonstrates how healthcare organizations pull in innovation from other industries and weave in support and expertise from the parent company in order to make innovation happen.

LEARN FROM BCBSMA: FINDING ITS SOUL IN HUMAN-CENTERED DESIGN

When we surveyed healthcare organizations about their progress on the shift to pervasive innovation, very few reported doing well. In fact, only 14 percent of providers and 15 percent of pharma companies believe they have made the Fourth Shift, while not a single payer reported having done so—most likely because payers have to completely shift their perspective on their role within the health system. Some payers are fighting that resistance to innovation by using both separate internal functions and external thought partnerships to propel innovative efforts. That combination of methods helps spread innovation throughout the organization.

When Robin Glasco started at Blue Cross Blue Shield of Massachusetts as Chief Innovation Officer, her mandate was to expand upon the organization's long history of innovation through the formation of a dedicated team. At the time, BCBSMA was one of the few Blue plans without a dedicated innovation team. A lot of innovative activity was happening in the competitive landscape, and BCBSMA wanted to increase its focus on weaving the discipline of innovation into the fabric of the organization. "We define innovation not as a thing but as a continuous state of reimagining what is possible—with the mission of transforming how we deliver health care. Our house in the future won't operate like our house in the past," says CEO Andrew Dreyfus. "Everything—from the plumbing

---

52   https://www.bayer.com/en/bayer-lifescience-ihub.aspx

and the wiring to the design and the fact that it's even like a house with four walls, a roof and windows—will change."

Glasco and her innovation team were charged with three key tasks: First, to bring the science and discipline of innovation into the culture of the organization, with the focus on human-centered design brought to life through experiential learning (e.g. crash courses, special sessions and boot camps). Second, the team is responsible for bringing human-centered design to large-scale initiatives to bring a different approach to solving existing business challenges. The third is to constantly disrupt and stay ahead of the competition.

To achieve those mandates, Glasco formed the internal innovation function, which hosts training and boot camps throughout the year to teach those involved in the organization how to carry innovation into other departments. Nearly 100 people from both inside and outside the company attend the immersive boot camp, where they learn about and apply human-centered design. Glasco and her team walk attendees through the multiple stages of innovation (e.g. empathy, problem definition, ideation, prototyping) and explore the necessary mindsets (e.g. action orientation and radical collaboration). Attendees leave the two-day session having identified what human-centered design is, what its value is, how it is applied and, most importantly, where they can use it in their work. The boot camp is also impactful because BCBSMA associates are joined by external participants such as students, professors, physicians and CEOs are exposed to new ways of thinking about and applying innovation. "We don't define innovation as a noun or a verb. We define it as a mindset of continuously reimagining what is possible. It requires us to embrace a bias toward action, collaboration with different minds, and a culture of prototyping. We must take a new look at the deep-rooted challenges in a highly complex healthcare ecosystem. That's innovation – it's more than a two-day boot camp," Glasco says.

In early 2018, BCBSMA also kicked off its first external innovation council of cross-industry business leaders. The Innovation Council focuses on two areas: radical collaboration and the belief that the answers to healthcare are hidden in plain sight in other industries. The Innovation Council is comprised of 30 external members and six BCBSMA employees. The team meets quarterly, and helps set the organization's disruption innovation agenda, designates someone to work with BCBSMA offline, in between the council meetings, and helps with co-design. The team is highly diverse, with transportation officials, government agents and technology experts to name a few. The council provides BCBSMA with different perspectives on the needs of consumers. While the team is in its early stages, it is already beginning to tackle the business challenge of moving away from fee-for-service and embracing the whole consumer.

CONCLUSION: INJECTING INNOVATION INTO EVERY DEPARTMENT

When healthcare organizations put innovation at the heart of how they serve consumers, they can better serve consumers in a relevant and engaging way. Just as Sephora combined its digital and in-store experiences, healthcare organizations can pursue innovation that increases cohesion and enhances the clinical experience. Experience and engagement innovation will strengthen the relationship of healthcare organizations with consumers, even in light of financial and digital changes on the horizon, and increase engagement for outcome improvement. Innovation is no easy task, as organizations face many barriers; but there are a few different routes to success. Let's review the takeaways:

MVP Accelerates Progress

Organizations can take a page from tech companies and use the minimal viable product (MVP) approach to explore innovation. As we witnessed with Advocate's same-day mammography appointment program, starting small allows for trial and error and holds less risk than full overhauls. To identify where to begin, organizations can map the journey, identify the greatest pain points and, given the resources available, determine the minimum model needed to prove impact.

Internal Startups Catalyze Innovation

Forming an internal startup, or incubator, can protect experience and engagement innovation from bureaucracy and red tape and, instead, propel it forward. As we saw with Boehringer Ingelheim's digital lab, innovation mindsets and design thinking are not incompatible with healthcare. They just sometime require a different environment. The agile environment and talent of a startup, paired with the resources and industry knowledge of a healthcare organization, can lead to powerful developments that reimagine the consumer experience.

External Sources Lead to New Ideas

Organizations should abandon the "invented here" mindset and widen their aperture to consider the capabilities and expertise of other players. We see healthcare innovation continuing to emerge from other industries and presenting an opportunity for investment for organizations with financial means. Furthermore, as we saw with BCBSMA's Innovation Council, consulting members of other industries can broaden an organization's understanding of consumers and the innovation needed to engage them.

The Fifth Shift

From Insights as a Department to a Culture of Consumer Obsession

"Maturing our organization in its consumer centricity is about listening to our members and acknowledging what they are saying with action. It's about integrating their voice into ours."
—**Doug Cottings, Staff Vice President,**
Market Strategy & Insights, Anthem

n our first four shifts, we discussed the importance of developing an experience strategy, connecting ecosystems, personalizing experiences and driving pervasive innovation. Making these shifts hinges on knowing what the consumer needs and wants and incorporating that into strategic and tactical decision-making to ultimately drive consumer preference and engagement. "At the end of the day, it is a competitive market place and everybody has choice. If we want to be their choice, we have to understand our customers deeply – where they are today; what tensions they face; and, how best to deliver solutions and experiences that relieve those tensions in the most relevant way," says Veronica Chase, Vice President of Marketing at Eli Lilly and Co. "If marketers do not deeply understand their customers and relentlessly focus on delivering upon a brand promise that meets their customer's needs, we cannot expect to be nor will we be their choice." In the Fifth Shift, we explore how organizations can build what we call an Insights Operating System (IOS), a system whose function is to help organizations get to the right insights, drive the right decisions at the right time and win with the right consumers. Before we discuss how organizations can build this capability, we will look at how retail giant Amazon's devotion to consumer insights led to its unprecedented growth and success.

LEARN FROM AMAZON: INSIGHT MACHINES GENERATE MEANINGFUL LAUNCHES

The extent to which Amazon understands consumers is arguably what has fueled its relentless success. Through its impeccable insight into consumer needs, the retail giant has revolutionized traditional retail strategies and defined the entire online shopping experience, from holiday gifts to bookstores to grocery shopping. Amazon frequently launches new programs, builds new features and upgrades old services; and, almost without fail, these improvements meet a need that consumers themselves didn't realize they were missing. Every Amazon touchpoint is designed from the consumer's perspective, from seamless returns to speedy complaint responses. Pain points that consumers experience in other settings are frictionless at Amazon. Take Amazon Prime, the subscription service with guaranteed two-day shipping and music and video streaming access. Few would have guessed that consumers would jump at the opportunity to pay $119 a year to expedite their shopping experience, but Amazon did. Since its Prime launch, Amazon has continued to add relevant services to the subscription and, from 2013 to 2017, saw the number of members grow—more than tripling from 25 million to over 90 million.[53]

The reason Amazon can build offerings that are so relevant is that the company has its finger on the pulse of consumer needs. Amazon has built an organization with the talent and structure to support the collection and analysis of endless amounts of consumer data. From micro-level data like search history to macro-level information such as industry trends, Amazon analyzes consumer data to inform everything it does—from product development to assortments to pricing strategies to its recent successes in entertainment. Being able to anticipate and predict consumer needs at an exponential rate has allowed Amazon to enter businesses that no one saw coming, from logistics to entertainment to groceries. The Amazon disintermediation effect has many executives wondering where Amazon will go next—with healthcare perhaps being the biggest target of all. None of this would be possible if Amazon hadn't evolved into a learning, insight-generating organization that anticipates and predicts both consumer and industry success and allows those insights to permeate the entire enterprise. Healthcare organizations, too, have an opportunity to anticipate consumer needs; but that will require the appropriate capabilities to bring those insights to life.

---

53   https://www.forbes.com/sites/louiscolumbus/2018/03/04/10-charts-that-will-change-your-perspective-of-amazon-primes-growth/#24cf248e3fee

THE CHALLENGE FOR HEALTHCARE: INSIGHTS ARE TRAPPED IN THE WRONG PLACES

Companies like Netflix, Spotify and Amazon were created to harness and leverage consumer insights to inform the development of relevant products, services and experiences. Healthcare organizations were not. Rather, healthcare organizations were designed to meet a basic human need—and the extent to which they engaged consumers in meeting that need has had little impact on their success. Now that healthcare organizations are responsible for lowering costs and driving consumer engagement and satisfaction, it is imperative that they understand consumers in a way they never have before. Healthcare organizations need to become insight machines. Given their legacy, however, many do not have the right teams, processes, skill-sets or tools for developing and leveraging insights as a strategic asset.

Insights as a strategic asset is the primary reason why Novant Health has invested so much in building its own Amazon version of a consumer-insights machine: constantly listening. "We are deliberate about having conversations with consumers and letting them define what remarkable care is—in their eyes," says Carl Armato, CEO. "We shouldn't try to figure it out or guess on our own. We should listen and then act."

When healthcare organizations invest in gathering the right insights, they sometimes uncover unexpected breakthroughs that influence decision-making in a way that is good for both the consumer and the business. Take global pharmaceutical company Amgen for example. To better support patients on Enbrel, Amgen's blockbuster biologic for moderate to severe rheumatoid arthritis, the company needed to find a way to help patients track their symptoms to assess their individual progress. To address this, initially the concept of building an app was considered. However, instead of relying on intuition, Amgen conducted targeted consumer insights research with Enbrel users to uncover what they would find most helpful. The research revealed that Enbrel users did not want to track symptoms via an app. They wanted something simple, like the ability to respond to text messages.

This insight lead to STATWISE™, a program in which patients receive daily texts to which they reply with a numerical answer assessing their morning stiffness, pain, and fatigue. These responses are then sent to the patient in a visually simple report. The patient can share this data with family, caregivers and/or bring the report to his or her next doctor appointment. The program has strengthened physician and patient dialogue. "The user-experience team took what could have been a very fancy, complex system and created something far more basic to make it easier for patients. The entire design and launch was influenced by consumer insights about what they were truly looking for," says Dave Marek, Vice President and General Manager, Neuroscience at Amgen.

The STATWISE™ story demonstrates that uncovering and acting upon deep consumer insights can be the key to reimagining the relationship that consumers have with health organizations and possibly the key to unlocking greater engagement.

INSIGHTS FOR ALL: BUILD YOUR NEW IOS

To become insight-driven, organizations must be able to surface relevant consumer knowledge that will influence decision-making. The combination of knowledge and action forms the IOS, an organizational structure that is equal parts consumer-insight processes and outcome-oriented decisions.

Insights Operating System (IOS) Defined

Knowledge

Organizations need to develop the capability to uncover consumer insights

Action

Once insights have been uncovered, organizations need mechanisms in place to act on them and incorporate into decision making

The center of the IOS is where relevant knowledge is uncovered and where a team with the right capabilities and processes sits. Once the insights team has developed the capability to identify the right knowledge, the next step is to equip the organization to act. Action requires mechanisms and processes for sharing information and for making consumer insights foundational for all decision-making. Some of those mechanisms are ongoing; others are more targeted and less frequent in order to draw attention to the most important insights. Both parts of the IOS are critical to its success. "It is a bit like football. You can have a fantastic quarterback; but if no one is open and ready to receive the ball, the game goes nowhere," says Prophet's Global Insights Partner, Christine Brandt Jones.

The two parts of the IOS work in conjunction to build a consumer-obsessed culture, with everyone from the CEO to the systems manager working on behalf of the consumer. If insights are uncovered but employees aren't trained to incorporate them into decision-making, though, then insights go unused. Likewise, if employees are committed to making decisions grounded in insights but are left without the right information, decisions will be made on assumptions. Either way, the result is the same: suboptimal experiences and disappointing business results. In the next chapter, "Creating a Consumer-Centric Culture," we explore how to cultivate effective consumer obsession. But first, let's look at the knowledge and actions required to drive the culture forward.

THE FIRST LAYER OF IOS: SURFACE THE RIGHT DATA

Consumer insights don't appear overnight or stand out in a large data set. They are formed through complex analysis, deriving meaning from large, diverse data sources. Identifying consumer insights requires the work of an experienced team that understands how data becomes an insight and how an insight turns into action. This is the first part of the IOS.

A strong insights team, say from a CPG company like Procter & Gamble, understands the process and effort required to uncover deep and meaningful insights from raw data. They know that a data point is essentially meaningless until it is given context. Once in the appropriate context, the data point becomes information that can be organized and structured for strategic usage. That information becomes knowledge when it is given meaning and implications, at which point it becomes a business learning. Knowledge becomes insight when it solves a problem and can be integrated and actionable. Until that point, data does not offer the organization its full value. As famous British journalist Miles Kington once said, "Knowledge is knowing that a tomato is a fruit. Wisdom is not putting it in a fruit salad." That type of understanding is commonplace in organizations accustomed to using data and insights as competitive tools, but it is not the norm at healthcare organizations. If organizations focus their efforts only on collecting data, they will not get to the wisdom necessary for turning insight into sound recommendations.

Translating insight into action requires a high-functioning team that understands how to contextualize, synthesize and derive meaning from disconnected sources of data. Organizations need more than a market research team that just collects data. They need a fully integrated and cohesive insights team. They need to interrogate data, investigate it and explore its implications. And that requires going beyond the obvious. Reading data helps an organization maintain its position in the market; uncovering insights allows the organization to *grow*. Through our work inside and outside healthcare, we have observed four different insight team archetypes: The Data Reactor, The 360 Reporter, The Business Strategist and The Culture Catalyst.

- **The Data Reactor** These teams operate at a basic level, conducting reactive project fulfillment research. They have limited connection to senior leaders. Their focus is on hindsight and tactical research and they have little involvement with functions beyond marketing. With a team like this, a healthcare organization cannot be consumer-obsessed and will struggle to engage consumers in new ways. These teams react but never anticipate. They report but rarely implement.

- **The 360 Reporter** This approach is slightly more advanced. These teams conduct both strategic and tactical research, integrating multiple sources of data to mine insights on individual behavior with a perspective on potential drivers of future behavior. This team represents the consumer to senior executives, sharing interesting trends and insights from the research but having a limited role in strategic decision-making. These teams focus more on storytelling and less on behavior changing.

- **The Business Strategist** These teams also present the voice of the consumer to senior executives, but their role is more advanced. They are present during planning and decision-making. The knowledge of the team spans across the entire organization, and these teams are sought out enablers for tackling big strategic challenges.

- **The Culture Catalyst** These strategic insights teams have extensive involvement and responsibility across functions and a direct line of sight into the executive suite. Their knowledge base helps drive the organization forward by focusing on both insight and foresight. These teams are part of the strategic planning process and help set the agenda on which initiatives are highest priority. The work of these teams and their profile are integral to driving both three- to five-year strategic plans and world-class consumer experiences.

Insight Operation System (IOS) Maturity Levels

BASIC   *ADVANCED*

The Data Reactor	The 360 Reporter	The Business Strategist	The Culture Catalyst
These teams operate at a basic level, conducting reactive project fulfillment research. They have limited connection to senior leaders.	*This approach is slightly more advanced, and teams conduct both strategic and tactical research, integrating multiple sources of data to mine insights on individual behavior with a perspective on potential drivers of future behavior.*	*In this model, teams also present the voice of the consumer to senior executives, but their role is more advanced and they are present during planning and decision-making.*	*This strategic insights team has extensive involvement and responsibility across functions and a direct line of sight into the executive suite. Their knowledge base helps drive the organization forward by focusing on both insight and foresight.*
Their focus is on hindsight and tactical research and they have little involvement with functions beyond marketing. With a team like this, a healthcare organization cannot be consumer-obsessed and will struggle to engage consumers in new ways. These teams react, never anticipate. They report, but rarely implement.	*This team represents the consumer to senior executives to share interesting trends and insights from the research, but this team has a limited role in strategic decision making. They focus more on storytelling and less on behavior changing.*	*The knowledge of this team spans across the entire organization and they are sought out enablers for tackling big strategic challenges.*	*They are a part of strategic planning and help to set the agenda on what initiatives are highest priority. Their work and profile are integral to driving both three-to-five-year strategic plans and world-class consumer experiences.*

Organizations that want to build a consumer-obsessed culture should aim to be Business Strategists or Culture Catalysts; however, most live as Data Reactors or 360 Reporters. When we surveyed healthcare organizations about the role of their current market research/insights team, only 12 percent responded that their insights team was able to catalyze culture change. Organizations must broaden that role beyond reactive market research if they want to make the shift and begin building the capabilities that will lead to understanding consumers on an individual level.

The Journey to Becoming a Culture Catalyst

Culture Catalysts have, over time, mixed the right blend of star talent, capabilities and processes to uncover the knowledge necessary to build relevant services and offerings and drive long-term strategies. It is a long road to becoming a Culture Catalyst, and understanding where you are today will go a long way in understanding the gap you need to fill.

No doubt, an insights team should have the expertise to conduct advanced analysis to uncover insights; but that skill is easy to teach. More difficult to teach are skills like problem definition and storytelling. Problem definition, often overlooked in the insights process, is a critical step. The better the team's grasp on the business problem they are working to solve, the better able they are to clarify the insights needed and where and how to find them. Clear problem definition is foundational to uncovering impactful insights. Take, for example, the goal of equal opportunity. Whether we define the problem as inequality or injustice has implications for research and will fundamentally change the approach to designing a solution. If we define the problem as inequality, then the solution is to give individuals the same opportunities. If we define the problem as injustice, the solution is to consider the specific situation of each individual and fill in the gaps between their opportunities and others' opportunities in order to create a level playing field.

Equality Doesn't Mean Justice

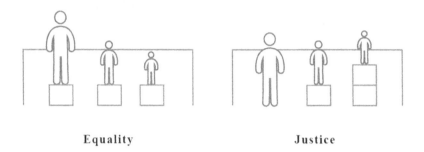

Equality   Justice

An example of this in healthcare is the Hospital Consumer Assessment of Healthcare Providers and Systems, or HCAHPS, the patient satisfaction survey required by all hospitals in the United States. If hospitals are trying to improve in patient satisfaction, then HCAHPS is a good measurement, as it evaluates specific areas such as food services, doctor communications and discharge preparation. If, however, hospitals want to improve overall satisfaction and build deeper, more engaged relationships, then HCAHPS is insufficient, as it fails to capture the holistic consumer experience and offers little insight into the state of an organization's relationship with its consumers.

Furthermore, the insights team needs to have employees with storyteller skills, as they will be responsible for sharing insights. The team needs to understand the context of the insight and weave together disparate pieces of information to tell a compelling story that will lead to a recommendation for how the insight can inform decision-making. Hiring talent with broader skills, beyond research, will move the insights team along the spectrum—away from the Data Reactor and on to the Culture Catalyst.

Processes Needed to Support Insight Development

In addition to acquiring talent with relevant capabilities for uncovering insights, organizations need to ensure that their teams have processes in place that support proactive insight development and not just reactive data collection. That requires building infrastructure that allows the team to gather consumer data and input by looking at the market from multiple angles. And that often involves developing a learning plan that identifies how and at what cadence the team will gather knowledge and connect it to the business. To develop a learning plan, the insights team should first compile any existing and accessible information (consumer data, competitive intelligence or market trends) and audit the current needs of the business and current projects in the works. Second, the team must determine where it makes the most sense to invest in insights by identifying objectives and strategies driven by data, then forming questions and hypothesis that are relevant. Finally, the team needs to prioritize and codify efforts, connecting insights to decision-making. That type of audit may lead to cutting certain projects—which is a good sign, because it typically means that the most impactful initiatives supported by insights get the proper funding and focus.

LEARN FROM AETNA: CONSOLIDATING INSIGHTS AND MARKETING MAGNIFIES VALUE

When Dave Edelman joined Aetna, he understood that insights would be critical to decision-making and effectively change member and enterprise behavior. Uncovering insights would require strengthening the organization's enterprise intelligence. At the time of his arrival, the marketing, branding and insights teams operated separately from each other, working in silos. Edelman consolidated their efforts under his leadership. Post-consolidation, Edelman evaluated the talent on his team to ensure they were up for the task and were aligned with the jobs they needed to accomplish. "You have to really look hard at your talent and ask: Is your talent going to take you there? Will they have the right strategic lens? Do they understand analytics and how to use analytics in what they do?" Edelman also took an active approach to ensure that his broader organization had the opportunity to shine. "Sometimes you have talent that is latent that needs to be unleashed," he says. "Early on, I gave people projects to own; and some really rose to the challenge. I could see that there was a lot more there to tap into."

This restructuring allowed the team to explore what it meant for Aetna to be member-facing and the implications that had for consumer experience and product design. Edelman also created Insight Ambassadors to work with other functions throughout the organization and collaborate on recommendations. Insight Ambassadors, which come from marketing, partner with business-unit leads to talk about the implications of consumer insights on the business and aligning them with strategic goals. "This team's role is to be senior advisor—as well as designers and executers of programs—and strategic counselors to the business, drawing on the insights. They need to take that work to the business unit and help [the business unit] understand how to use it," Edelman says. Today, Aetna's marketing, brand and insight functions are fully integrated and operating at a high level. Edelman's team is a Business Strategist on its way to becoming a Culture Catalyst. Armed with a deep understanding of members and connected to leaders and functions across the enterprise, the team plays an integral role in driving Aetna's strategy forward.

LEARN FROM LILLY: REWRITE THE JOB DESCRIPTION

Given the new demands of healthcare insights teams, some organizations have found that the talent they previously had for what would have been sufficient for a Data Reactor was no longer sufficient for the needs of the business. Dave Moore, Senior Director of Global Insights and Analytics at Lilly until late 2017, says that as Lilly began making concerted efforts to become more consumer-centric, it had to adjust its approach to recruiting and training insight talent. The global pharmaceutical company began to hire talent with skills in data synthesis, integrating data from multiple sources and with a high IQ for data-informed storytelling. Moore and his team realized that while the talent pools they previously recruited from were highly equipped to collect data, candidates often lacked the skills needed to translate this data into a story that provided deep insight into customers. Moore says his team started targeting individuals who had the thought process of a researcher (e.g. problem definition, data sourcing) paired with the ability to understand findings within a context and connect them back to customers and the business. Lilly also rotates people in and out of the insights function to ground them in the business, allowing them to eventually bring their consumer-focused lens to other functions throughout their rotations. Acquiring talent with a more strategic lens has helped Lilly's insights team move from Research Reporter to Business Strategist. The team's ability to capture market data and consider that data in the context of clinical findings and challenges has made the insight team an essential partner across the business-unit teams, providing both strategic and tactical guidance in solving business challenges.

THE SECOND LAYER OF IOS: TURN INSIGHTS INTO ACTION

Even if an organization uncovers groundbreaking insights, those insights are helpful only if the rest of the organization can act on them. Anthem's Doug Cottings explains that action is the next frontier for his team, which began as a pure Data Reactor and has evolved into a 360 Reporter. Since Cottings joined Anthem, the team has gained a deeper understanding of the member experience and has established a VOC platform to host a wide variety of data— from demographic and claims data to data about what hold music the member hears or how long the member was actually on hold. The team, however, has yet to unlock its full strategic potential. "The action side is where we need improvement, harvesting our new knowledge for fundamental changes in the member experience," says Cottings. "We can play a more consultative role, but that will require democratizing the VOC so everyone has access to it."

This is where the second part of the IOS comes into play. All too often, research is conducted or data is gathered but never used—not because it wasn't insightful, but because the data didn't make it into the hands of people who could use it at the right time. We have found three key ways to disseminate insights: self-service mechanisms, targeted communications and formal or informal cross-functional partnerships.

Turning Insights Into Action

Self-service mechanisms

Targeted communications

Formal or informal cross-functional partnerships

Self-Service Mechanisms

To ensure that insights are available cross-functionally, organizations can establish dashboards and portals that are regularly updated with relevant data and analysis. Lilly, for example, has a knowledge-management hub that houses the research conducted over the past 12 years. The hub contains key summaries, visuals and lessons for every business or therapeutic area. The hub gives other functions an essence of what the organization knows about consumers now and how this knowledge has evolved over time. Other organizations have similar insight dashboards. Data experts recommend self-service dashboards for certain performance indicators so that updating reports is seamless for the core team and the information is available on-demand and in transparent ways. Novant Health, for example, has an insights dashboard that is available to the broader organization.

Targeted Communications

Having an ongoing database of insights is good, but organizations should also establish processes to call out key insights. Those communications become an opportunity to spell out implications for business goals and highlight key changes in the market. On a quarterly basis, Lilly issues a newsletter full of research and insight updates, which is a direct way for the team to communicate its most recent findings and highlight key insights. Sometimes the team conducts the updates live to demonstrate how the insights align with key priorities.

Perhaps even more powerful than a newsletter or a town hall are Lilly's immersive insights sessions. Lilly believes the best way to bring insights to life is through employees who have an appreciation for the consumers they serve, and the challenges they face in dealing with and managing their conditions. Lilly inspires this appreciation by holding live workshops in which insights are brought to life through immersive experiences. Employees from different business functions walk through showrooms and see how consumer insights and consumer segments play out in the real life of customers. They meet patients who are invited in to talk about their condition. These sessions are an engaging way to make customer needs more deeply understood, using context and immersive exercises. "When employees get to see insights through the eyes of the patient it becomes real. It leads to greater appreciation and understanding of the work we do and the importance of the patient's voice in our work," says Moore.

Other companies also use this technique. Sprint, for example, hosts an insights road show with the most senior business owners. Sprint shows the owners the consumer data, explains what the data can do and asks what problems it could help solve. Sprint demonstrates on site how insights can help solve business challenges and deliver results. "We learned that people really value the facts that allow them to drive results, so we focused just on delivering facts—not opinions. What we've been able to do is lay intelligence and facts over people's personal experience," says Sprint's Chief Digital Officer, Rob Roy.[54]

Cross-Functional Partnership

At organizations like Novant Health, where the data and analytics capability is still in the building process, cross-functional teams consult the insights team to learn exactly how insights might be used. The process began when Mathias Krebs, Senior Director, Insights & Analytics, would approach teams to learn about the challenges they faced and solve those issues using insights. Over time, Krebs and his team built a reputation for both understanding the problems and then delivering and incorporating the insights that would help most. The demand throughout Novant Health for an Insights & Analytics partnership and guidance has steadily risen under Krebs' leadership. While the process is largely informal, it has allowed for close partnerships—with insights used in the most effective ways.

---

54   https://www.mckinsey.com/business-functions/digital-mckinsey/our-insights/how-to-build-a-data-first-culture

"The demand for insights has grown organically," says Krebs. "It is informal at the moment, but teams come to us because they understand the value of the knowledge we hold and the ways we can help them."

As we have seen, organizations often have parts of an insights capability in place. Other organizations, however, are taking a holistic approach to changing the way they understand their consumers. When Stacey Geffken, Director of Product Development and Market Research, joined Geisinger Health Plan, the market research function was firmly a Data Reactor. The team primarily evaluated the organization's performance in the market and occasionally conducted focus groups. "Essentially, the team started as a small group of people just debating what they thought the consumer wanted," says Geffken. Chris Fanning, Chief Marketing Officer, brought on Geffken to improve that function, because Fanning believes that consumer insights need to be integral to the way the organization develops products and experiences. "Consumer centricity cannot be viewed simply as a marketing piece. It has to be tied to all strategic goals," says Fanning.

Change started first by bringing consumers into Geisinger offices to share, first-hand, what their experience with the Geisinger Plan looked like. From there, Geffken and her team established a baseline of consumer understanding by routinely collecting structured feedback about the experience, implementing NPS, conducting an annual key driver study and developing touchpoint surveys to build out a voice of the customer platform. The team has greatly improved the efficiency of solving consumer pain points and has given member experience teams greater insight into how they can better serve members.

The Geisinger Health Plan insights team straddles the role of 360 Reporter and Strategist. To move into a greater strategic role, Geffken will have to build the capability for more leaders and managers to view consumers holistically to allow the organization to view the experience across both the payer and provider. "Insights should be much more powerful in an integrated system like ours, because we have greater access to the consumer's healthcare experience across the entire member and patient healthcare continuum," says Geffken. "We have an opportunity here, and that's what we are building toward."

Geisinger Health Plan isn't the only organization that uses multiple tools for acting on insights. Cigna does the same. Consumer insights play an important and integrated role in strategy, because of the organization's strong operating system and skillfully hired staff. Cigna's Insights That Matter operating system is based on a formal process of identifying business problems to be solved, identifying the necessary questions to be answered, finding clarity around the measures the company seeks to move and then identifying relevant insights that are needed to address those measures. To ensure that the entire business is using the insights in decision-making, the team runs a number of programs—from town halls throughout the organization to workshops to align the organization—and shares use cases and early findings. Importantly, Global Chief Marketing Officer Lisa Bacus, whose background includes a similar role at Ford Motor Co., has a seat at the table with Cigna's CEO to ensure that insights play a key role in decision-making. "We started with a vision to deliver on our mission of improving the health, well-being and sense of security for those we serve and on bringing a data-driven and insights-led approach to all we do," says Bacus.

CONCLUSION: SHARE INSIGHTS FREELY, THEN HARNESS THEM FOR GROWTH

When an organization builds a strong IOS, with a well-equipped insights team and mechanisms for distributing insights across the organization, it will be better prepared to cultivate a culture of consumer obsession. In the next chapter, we explore how to foster that obsession and put customers on center stage. Before we explore that, though, let's review the key lessons from this shift:

Uncovering Insights Leads to Growth

To move an insights team from Data Reactor to Culture Catalyst, organizations need to reevaluate the talent on their insights teams. Organizations need to evaluate their current talent and move toward a recruiting process like Lilly's, which focuses on finding more strategically minded individuals. What skills and expertise do these individuals have? Can they both evaluate the current state and identify opportunities for growth?

An Insight Without a Home Is Meaningless

As we saw with Cottings' team at Anthem, a strong IOS requires putting processes and systems in place that allow for the sharing of insights across the organization. Organizations should audit its current processes for distributing insights to the appropriate functions and leaders. Are those processes comprehensive and intuitive? Do they enhance the organization's ability to understand and incorporate insights? Processes that may work include insight dashboards, newsletter updates or immersive workshops.

Insight-Driven Organizations Are Disciplined Organizations

Insights do not easily make their way into decision-making, especially in healthcare organizations where decisions born out of assumption are all too common. As we saw with Amgen's development of STATWISE™, organizations must be deliberate in their incorporation of insights to uncover opportunities for growth. Establishing official processes, procedures and protocol around the decision-making process can be one place to start.

Creating a
Consumer-Centric Culture

"Every step we take, every tactical strategic decision we make, is based on what is in the best interest of the patient—and that is the only interest to be considered. At Mayo Clinic, we put patients first. That is the foundation of our culture."
—John Noseworthy, M.D., CEO, Mayo Clinic

As we have explored throughout this book, the healthcare industry is in flux. Rising expectations from consumers and changing reimbursement models are pushing organizations to engage collaboratively with the e-consumer. That requires providers to reconsider the old philosophy that dictates that the physician controls the dialogue or the traditional definitions of consumer satisfaction that focus on touchpoints. Instead, the focus must turn to aggressively pursuing consumer relationships built on partnership and collaboration. Payers and pharma companies must also engage consumers and drive greater outcomes. "We pride ourselves on our best-in-class customer service, but realize that we can't rest on our laurels," says Blue Cross Blue Shield of Massachusetts CEO Andrew Dreyfus. "As the marketplace and customer expectations evolve, we know we need to constantly re-evaluate our products, services and technology to ensure that we keep our members at the center of everything we do." If healthcare organizations are to serve the e-consumer and engage, empower and equip them, they, too, will need to make a shift and put the consumer at the center of all they do—including, most importantly, their culture.

It is important to keep in mind that using the term "consumer-centric" to describe their culture is not widely accepted at healthcare organizations. Most executive leaders in the industry still use the term "patient-centric" to describe their culture. Their focus is on caring for the patients who seek their services, and that focus is sacred within medicine. While we prefer to use the term "consumer" to establish the importance of the entire healthcare journey, and we believe that organizations are headed in that direction, the executives with whom we spoke for this chapter use the term "patient."

What Is a Consumer-Obsessed Culture?

Consumer-obsessed organizations embrace the consumer from the top of the organization to the bottom. The consumer always comes first. Amazon is arguably the greatest example of this with its three key tenets: the empty chair, the "working-backwards" philosophy and leadership role modeling.

Everything Amazon does revolves around consumer insights. That obsession began during Amazon's earliest days, when CEO Jeff Bezos would famously bring an empty chair to executive meetings to represent the consumer—the most important person in the room. The empty chair set Amazon's precedent that the consumer should always be at the center of all the company does and to have a seat at the head of the table. Today, the organization continues to find ways to make consumer obsession permeate the organization, from its 2009 acquisition of Zappos to its mandate that every manager spend a minimum of two days in a call center, interacting one-on-one with consumers.

Amazon weaves consumer obsession into the product-development process through its "working backwards" philosophy. At a very high level, that requires development teams to identify a consumer need, analyze it, determine the necessary steps for addressing it and work out the logistics—all before launching into development. The process also requires teams to create a hypothetical press release for the idea, along with a six-page set of FAQs. That forces teams to clarify the objective of the idea and articulate it in a way that others can understand without ambiguity. Also, the directives don't just move through inboxes; rather, they are socialized internally with the energy warranted for an official launch date. Amazon does not invest in development and then vie for consumer buy-in. Amazon begins with the consumer and ends with the consumer. While Amazon's tactics may seem like simple concepts, those deliberate moves weave consumer obsession into the culture—and it pays off: Amazon currently ranks as the third-most-relevant brand in the United States in Prophet's Brand Relevance Index and lands in the top 10 brands in the United Kingdom and Germany.

Fostering Consumer Obsession in Healthcare

Amazon's approach is a model for how healthcare organizations can meaningfully partner with their consumers. For organizations to make progress toward becoming consumer-centric requires a collective understanding that strategy and culture must work together to move the entire organization forward. Strategy includes direction and actions, while culture includes motivations and behaviors. A strong culture motivates organizations to operate differently and inspire organic behavioral change, while strategy reinforces consumer centricity by defining the capabilities and actions required. Incorporating consumer centricity in the culture of an organization, from the janitor to the chief medical officer, is equally important to bringing the organization to life strategically.

To be clear, most healthcare organizations believe they put the patient first. Putting the consumer first is different. Patient-first thinking gets trapped in the exam and operating rooms. Consumer-first thinking extends to the before and after interactions with healthcare; it values the consumer voice throughout the whole journey. Extending patient-first thinking to consumer-first thinking isn't an easy task and often demands that employees change their fundamental understanding of whom they serve. The Mayo Clinic's CEO and President John Noseworthy, M.D., explains that as his organization has broadened the view of "the patient" to mean "the consumer," there have been cultural roadblocks—and overcoming those roadblocks has even required the contextualization of consumer-centric within patient-centric. "When you try to introduce a new idea to the organization, you are likely to face resistance," says Dr. Noseworthy. "But if you can put the idea in the context of patient-centered care, they will love it and innovate around it."

This chapter covers ways for organizations to build a consumer-obsessed culture. Developing a strong culture is not something that happens entirely organically, even in the best companies. It requires a concerted effort. "Driving a strong culture is an everyday thing," says Bill Valle, CEO at Fresenius Medical Care North America. "It will be a journey that will last a lifetime. It's a commitment from the top to the bottom, reminding everybody, every day, why we're here.

Whether it's a direct patient care associate or someone in finance or IT, everyone has to understand that their job directly connects to those we care for."

In the First Shift, we discussed defining consumer centricity as part of a holistic experience strategy. That definition must have the support of all employees. They must understand it and live it. We have found three key strategies to help maximize consumer centricity cultural success:

Inspire employees by mobilizing them around the organization's definition of consumer centricity so that they own it, believe in it and embrace it.

Enable employees to succeed in becoming consumer-centric by providing them with the tools, resources and support they need to succeed.

Incentivize employees to change their mindset, which is critical; understanding what those right incentives are even more critical.

There are several different ways to tackle each of the three approaches, and organizations will need to determine which approach will be most impactful for their employees. An organization that uses a combination of the three approaches will be better equipped to move along the five shifts and deliver a consumer-centric experience.

The Consumer-Centric Culture Change Playbook

INSPIRE PEOPLE	ENABLE PEOPLE	INCENTIVIZE PEOPLE
Inspiring employees by mobilizing them around the organization's definition of consumer centricity so that they own it, believe in it and embrace it	*Enabling employees to succeed in becoming consumer-centric by providing them with the tools, resources and support they need to succeed*	*Incentivizing employees to change their mindset is critical; understanding what those right incentives are is even more critical*
1 Leadership role modeling	1 Create new working environments	1 Incentivize personally
2 Codify cultural expectations	2 Reimagine traditional business functions	2 Incentivize professionally
3 Co-create cultural expectations	3 Put purpose over process	3 Incentivize financially
4 Make it personal		

INSPIRE THE TEAM

Healthcare organizations may have a vision of where they want to go, but they need internal support to get there. "We didn't develop a consumer- and patient-centric strategy for the sake of hanging it up on the wall," says Kevin Brown, President and CEO of Piedmont Healthcare. "The patient is at the center of all that we do. We're living and breathing it. It is how we manage, run meetings, prioritize initiatives, approve capital, hire talent. Everything ties back to it." Consumer-centric transformation must be activated at the ground level, and healthcare organizations can successfully inspire their employees in several ways; for example, demonstrate leadership role modeling, codify cultural expectations, co-create cultural expectations and make it personal.

Leadership Teams Need to Model Consumer-Centric Behaviors

Inspiring employees to embrace consumer centricity requires vocal leaders, starting at the top, who demonstrate that priority through their actions. Bill Valle says they are making concerted efforts at Fresenius to hire leaders who embrace consumer centricity and let go of leaders who don't. "Our special sauce is starting at the very top of the organization. If this culture doesn't feel right for you, if you prefer to stay in the old world, this isn't the place for you. We have set very clear expectations for my senior leadership team. They gauge the behavioral clock for the rest of the organization," he says. It is important to have leaders who are on board with pursuing consumer centricity, as their behaviors set a precedent for the broader organization.

Other organizations focus on building teams that have experience developing consumer-centric behaviors. Intermountain Healthcare, for example, hired Kevan Mabbutt as Chief Consumer Officer. Mabbutt was previously Global Head of Consumer Insight at The Walt Disney Company, one of the most consumer-oriented companies in the world. He also worked at the Discovery Channel and the BBC. Mabbutt is responsible for representing the voice of the consumer at the highest levels. By hiring someone to model a consumer-first perspective, Intermountain communicated that consumer centricity was a top priority.

Articulate Cultural Expectations

Much like an organization's definition of consumer centricity, a consumer-obsessed culture is most impactful when outlined in a tangible manner and built into the organization's processes. By articulating the culture through behavioral expectations, organizations can help employees understand what consumer centricity means to them and what it looks like when carried out on a day-to-day basis.

LEARN FROM ABBVIE: MAKING "REMARKABLE" ITS NORTH STAR

When AbbVie, the former specialty pharmaceutical division of Abbott, was spun off to create a new $18 billion company, it was faced with transforming a historically deliberate organization into an agile biopharmaceutical company. Overcoming that challenge would require both a new strategy and a new culture.

To create that culture, AbbVie developed a program called "The AbbVie Way," with three pillars to define how the organization approaches its work, its capabilities and the "remarkable" impact it will have. "One of the things I've learned is that people need clear strategies and clear intent," Tim Richmond, Senior Vice President, Human Resources at AbbVie, explains in *Profile Magazine*. "Ultimately, our mission is to deliver a consistent stream of innovative medicines that can address unmet health needs. That's really our North Star." Those pillars tie in to how the new organization will operate in a consumer-centric manner. "Everything comes back to having a remarkable impact on our patients' lives. If we can do that, the business will succeed," he says.

To activate its cultural transformation, AbbVie invested in mobilizing employees across the organization through "The AbbVie Way," which employed a decentralized, global team of ambassadors, a series of workshops and a journey-map exercise that provided an interactive way for employees to feel personally connected to the vision. Furthermore, "The AbbVie Way" articulates specific principles for how the company expects work to get done, informing both processes and systems and the organization's approach to talent, including hiring and incentives. AbbVie has made impressive progress in establishing its culture since its spin-off from Abbott in 2013. The organization's annual employee survey reveals that employee engagement scores near 80 percent, almost a 10 percent increase from 2013. Employees also gave the organization's culture a high score of 74 percent in 2016, up from 60 percent in 2013. Today, AbbVie continues to invest in order to both strengthen its culture and deliver on strategic priorities in support of its goal of making a remarkable impact on consumers' lives.

Creating the Human Experience at Novant Health

Novant Health defines culture by taking elements of the consumer experience and applying them to employees. "We don't look at the patient experience separately from the physician/team member experience," says CEO Carl Armato. "They are blended together. We need to create a remarkable experience for our patients and our team members." The "human experience" comes to life in the "People Credo," which outlines specific behaviors and expectations for the Novant Health team. From recruitment and retention to growth and development protocol, the People Credo codifies the expectation that team members know each other, listen to each other, empower each other and lead each other. "Guided by the People Credo, we came up with new leadership development programs for physicians and nurses and administrators that brought a new resiliency and a reminder about why we do what we do with the patient at the center and deliver the remarkable experience people deserve," says Armato.

Tap Employees for New Definitions

In addition to articulating what consumer centricity means, employees must derive personal meaning from it. That is particularly important, as employees are often the ones who interact with consumers and care for patients on a daily basis. Leadership can help employees find that personal meaning through co-creation.

LEARN FROM INDIANA UNIVERSITY HEALTH: AFTER A MERGER, CO-CREATING THE FUTURE

Amid pressure from payers to shift from a fee-for-service to a fee-for-value model and a continued emphasis on accountable, effective care, Indiana University Health (IUH) had to re-think its business strategy and vision. To expand access, IUH bought and built primary-care providers, urgent-care centers and hospitals throughout the state and then faced the challenge of unifying those disparate operations.

That created two challenges. First, acquired employees were rolled into the organization but were not culturally assimilated to the ways of IUH. Second, IUH was changing expectations for old employees. Recognizing the need for post-merger integration, IUH leaders took the time to understand the needs, wants and aspirations, both personally and professionally, of the new employees. That helped IUH create a brand promise that was common to both its employees and members of the communities in which they lived. "We believe that it was critical for team members to be a part of the development of our promise. We want them to own it and to feel proud delivering on it," says Mike Yost, Vice President of Marketing, Outreach and Experience at IUH. In creating what would be called the IUH Promise, the organization conducted employee focus groups and co-creation sessions around the state, and employees ultimately selected from a range of options to determine which brand promise to adopt. "Not everyone got the old promise, particularly our professional staff. With this one, it feels like everyone gets it. Now it's like any good brand. Can we show that we're reinforcing this promise with actions and decisions? We have definite examples. We have to do it for every patient, every interaction. That's the next big step we're working through," says CEO Dennis Murphy.

To solidify its efforts, IUH spent a year rolling out the new promise and associated behaviors and values, carefully introducing them across the organization's 15 hospitals and 30,000 employees. By collaborating with employees throughout the system, IUH achieved two key things. First, IUH minimized friction between the medical and administrative staffs by creating the foundation for a culture that resonated with both. Second, by endorsing co-creation, IUH set the expectation that teamwork is essential.

Make Consumer-Centric Healthcare Personal

There is no question that healthcare is personal. Whether undergoing treatment or taking care of a sick loved one, we all experience healthcare at a deeply individual level. "Healthcare is a unifying factor for all Americans," says BCBSMA's Robin Glasco. "No matter how much money you make or where you live—whether you're paying claims, paying bills, seeing patients, writing regulations, enforcing regulations or trying to purchase policies—we are all greatly impacted."

Sometimes, organizations can make consumer centricity more powerful when leaders emphasize the personal aspect. That requires leaders to find their own source of inspiration and voice in their definition of consumer centricity so they can constantly remind the organization who they are serving each day, why their work matters and why the experience should be among the best in any category. Every CEO we interviewed emphasized his or her critical role in that endeavor.

LEARN FROM CLEVELAND CLINIC: UNCOVERING HEALTHCARE'S HEART

The Cleveland Clinic has made huge strides in making its vision feel personal to each employee. The organization produced a short video called, "Empathy: The Human Connection to Patient Care," which features patients, families and frontline employees grappling with the challenges of both the healthcare system and serious health issues. Originally meant for an internal audience, the video touched such a human chord that it went viral. The video asks the audience to put themselves in the shoes of patients and approach every interaction with empathy. "These videos have been pivotal in rallying people around a core element of our mission: to provide exceptional patient experiences, every day, to every single patient," Adrienne Boissy, M.D., Chief Experience Officer at Cleveland Clinic, told the *Harvard Business Review.*

Other organizations make consumer centricity personal by putting employees in direct contact with the consumers they serve. For example, global pharmaceutical company Pfizer offers employees a paid workday to participate in patient volunteer activities, giving employees the opportunity to gain a deeper understanding of how patients manage their conditions. "We have to put ourselves in the shoes of patients and make sure that everything we are doing, from drug development through market launch, is with the patient, front and center," says Angela Hwang, Group President of Pfizer Essential Health.

ENABLE SUCCESSFUL EMPLOYEES

Once an organization has inspired employees to embrace consumer centricity, they must be given the tools to carry out consumer centricity. In our discussions with healthcare executives, many voice the frustration of making consumer centricity a strategic priority that doesn't move forward, because it lacks sufficient support. As it stands now, old processes and systems established before the advent of consumer centricity often stand in the way of getting things done. Anthem's Chief Marketing and Consumer Officer, Patrick Blair, found this to be the case. "You can't go a day without seeing the newest shiny healthcare technology, but we realized we need to be brilliant at the basics," he says. Excelling at the basics required increasing access, convenience, transparency and trust for members and enabling frontline talent to do their jobs in a new way. "We should empower our agents to solve consumer needs without having to get a supervisor's approval…it is about doing the right thing." A consumer-obsessed culture needs employees who are enabled with the right training, skills and tools and who are empowered to act.

Organizations can go about enabling employees in a few different ways; for example, creating new working environments, reimagining traditional business functions and putting purpose over process.

Create Environments That Reinforce the Culture You Want

As healthcare continues to evolve, the demands of employees working at healthcare organizations need to evolve, as well. (And in some cases, change altogether.) Some organizations find they need entirely different people to carry out consumer centricity, and often that talent does not fit the mold of a traditional healthcare employee. Advocate Healthcare encountered that challenge when it attempted to increase its digital capabilities. Advocate was trying to hire new team members accustomed to working for *Fortune* 500 companies. But health systems have neither the money nor the working environments to match those of companies such as Google. To solve that challenge, Senior Vice President and Chief Marketing and Digital Officer Kelly Jo Golson spent time with companies like Google to understand and replicate some aspects of the culture that those organizations have created. As a result, Golson has been deliberate about creating situations that enable both digitally-minded and healthcare-minded people to thrive. She has offered satellite locations and provided the opportunity for people to work remotely so that they can be in a big-city environment rather than in Advocate headquarters, which is 25 miles outside Chicago. Golson also changed the working environment to mirror that of startups, with beanbags, white boards, special lighting and digital signage. "Healthcare continues to attract people who want to make a difference in other peoples' lives," she says, "and my hope is that, through these efforts, we will still find people driven by the mission of healthcare but also coupled with more digital strategy."

Encourage Employees to Make Consumer-Centric Decisions

An important part of consumer-obsession is demonstrating that commitment to consumers themselves, which requires empowering the employees who serve them directly. As part of its ongoing transformation from a health insurance company, which exists to manage payments and claims, to a health advocate that helps consumers achieve healthier lives, Florida Blue was guided by the principle of "first interaction resolution" as it revamped its customer-service function. That approach significantly augments the traditional first-call resolution, which can result in multiple transfers and frustrated consumers. The first interaction is critical, because it sets the foundation for a deeper relationship where consumers are engaged and more loyal. "We realized that we had to earn our way into relationships through first-interaction resolution," says Prakash Patel, M.D., who was Chief Operating Officer at GuideWell & Florida Blue and President of GuideWell Health before joining Anthem in August of 2018. "The number one reason why our customers get frustrated with us occurs when we don't answer their question the first time they ask. It sounds simple; but when questions and issues are taking multiple calls, hold times and representatives to solve, people get frustrated."

Florida Blue mapped out the consumer journey to develop a comprehensive approach for addressing consumers' questions at the first touchpoint. Florida Blue invested in systems that aggregate data across formerly disparate platforms so employees could be empowered with the right tools and information to answer questions, as well as offer solutions and value outside of the immediate issue at hand. The tools don't just enable employees to do their job; instead, they enable employees to do their job in service of the consumer, which ensures both internal and external impact.

Put Purpose Over Process

As healthcare organizations shift their mindset, they may find that the processes they have in place are not conducive to consumer centricity. Great processes, whether operational or strategic, should be informed by asking how the organization can deliver the best outcome for consumers. Starting with this question leads to clarity of purpose for building a consumer-centered organization. This purpose-first, process-second philosophy better enables employees to deliver on a consumer-centric strategy instead of being inhibited by legacy processes and protocols. The philosophy enabled a transformation at the Department of Veteran Affairs (VA). In 2014, the VA, which provides healthcare for more than nine million veterans in the United States, was in crisis. Widespread issues with wait times led to patient deaths and intense scrutiny from both Congress and the general public. Behind the chaos was a deep cultural problem.

Robert McDonald, Secretary of Veteran Affairs at the time, described the organization as "a culture of learned helplessness," one in which employees lacked both the tools and empowerment to bring consumer centricity to life. To change the culture, the VA revamped its processes to be driven by its purpose of serving veterans. With the purpose in place, the VA then designed processes and invested heavily in training and tools to articulate consumer centricity and enable and empower frontline employees at their 160-plus facilities to innovate in ways that deliver on the mission.

"Every employee should own what they do, and they should always have a personal project ongoing to improve what they do," says McDonald. Since 2014, the VA has made substantial progress. While it still has much work to do, a 2016 report from RAND found that the system outperformed the private sector on 96 percent of outpatient measures. Additionally, the VA has reduced pending claims by 90 percent. Healthcare organizations can empower employees to drive consumer centricity by ensuring process doesn't get in the way of progress (or purpose).

INCENTIVIZE THE TEAM

Once employees have embraced consumer centricity and have the tools to deliver it, they still may require an extra push to act. For some, cultural transformation is an enormous shift in their day-to-day lives. Organizations can help by incentivizing their employees and teams personally, professionally and financially.

Establish Metrics That Drive Change

Mobilizing around consumer centricity requires top-to-bottom alignment on common goals. Organizations need to establish clear metrics that reinforce consumer centricity to the overall business strategy. If organizations value and reward only non-consumer metrics like revenue or operating efficiency, then progress on those metrics is all that will be delivered. Having consumer metrics, even ones as simple as satisfaction, is critical to showing and driving a true commitment to consumer centricity. It changes employees' motivations and behaviors, which are both critical components culture.

Recognizing that consumer centricity must be viewed as a driver of growth, leaders are rethinking what they measure. Many organizations are moving from measures tied to satisfaction (e.g., Hospital Consumer Assessment of Healthcare Providers and System, NHS Patient Satisfaction Surveys) to measures tied to loyalty (e.g., Net Promoter Score, NPS). "Based on our market research and the consumerism movement, we believe that we need to move to a patient-loyalty metric as our ultimate success measure as opposed to the historic focus on patient satisfaction," says IUH's Mike Yost. "Patient satisfaction will continue to be highly important as it is foundational to loyalty; however, we need to raise the bar and understand how to create customer loyalty in healthcare. Based on our customer research, we are learning that we need to find new ways to connect with our patients and make the experience more personalized to them." Relationship metrics help paint a fuller picture of the experience and will compel functions across the organization to establish ways of working that address the experience holistically.

Link New Strategies to People's Pay

Another way organizations can encourage employees to embrace consumer centricity is through incentives. Putting compensation and promotions on the line is a sure-fire way to change behavior that, in turn, will foster a new culture.

In 2014, health insurer Anthem made consumer centricity one of three strategic priorities. To set a foundation for change, Anthem looked at its key metrics and realized that, while consumer-centric measures were in place, the organization lacked clarity around creating real change. In 2015, executive leadership endorsed NPS as its key metric and tied it to executive compensation, resulting in a focus on relationship building with consumers. Initially, NPS accounted for five percent of compensation in 2016; it increased to 10 percent in 2017.

However, that was not the end of the journey. "Once it affected everyone's bonus, the demand to meet with the leaders and their teams to discuss the metric took off," says Doug Cottings, Staff Vice President, Market Strategy & Insights at Anthem. "Those wanting to understand the results, how NPS is measured and what actions each department can take to improve surged dramatically and continue to increase." Even with strong executive alignment and the program in place, there was significant work to be done in implementing NPS throughout the organization and sharing results to keep up the momentum. As Anthem found, incentives on their own are not enough to drive results. Instilling lasting cultural change requires that employees have a clear understanding of specific performance objectives, behaviors and actions needed to drive improvements tied to consumer centricity.

Other organizations are taking similar measures to drive home the importance of consumer centricity. GlaxoSmithKline (GSK) became the first pharmaceutical company to fundamentally revamp its incentive structure for its U.S. sales teams, moving from the number of prescriptions issued to more consumer-centric metrics. Today, GSK incentivizes sales representatives based on three factors: individual knowledge, behaviors and activity; evaluations by customers; and overall business performance. The change was made as part of the organization's "Patient First" program, which focuses on facilitating better collaboration between GSK and the broader healthcare community. The change helps GSK promote a culture that values patient interests over financial interests and that allows frontline representatives to focus on knowing the products inside and out and delivering great service to the doctors and healthcare teams they serve.

CONCLUSION: THREE KEYS TO CULTURE CHANGE

While a culture shift is challenging, the stories from successful organizations that are fostering a consumer-obsessed culture demonstrate that there are tangible steps that organizations can take to get started. An organization that can nurture consumer obsession will be able to move along the five shifts more efficiently. With employees who understand, embrace and live consumer centricity, organizations can drive change and begin to build more engaging relationships with consumers. Let's review the three key parts of building a consumer-obsessed culture:

Mobilization Begins at the Top

With consumer centricity as a priority at the top, organizations need to inspire their teams to carry it out. Leaders at organizations should consider the ways in which they can promote consumer centricity. Some, like IUH's Dennis Murphy, may focus on role-modeling appropriate behaviors. Others, like Fresenius's Bill Valle, may concentrate on hiring talent committed to consumer centricity. Either way, leaders should be able to articulate consumer centricity and its implications for employees in a way that inspires employees and resonates with them on a personal level.

Tools and Processes to Make a Consumer-Centric Culture a Reality

Even if leaders set the stage for a consumer-centric mindset, an impact is possible only if employees have the tools and processes they need to carry out consumer centricity. Like Florida Blue, organizations can evaluate their most consumer-facing employees and audit the processes in place that enable those employees to do their jobs. Do those processes align with consumer centricity? What are the employee obstacles or pain points that hinder delivering a consumer-centric experience?

Living the Culture Requires an Extra Push

Cultural changes often require employees to change their daily approach to their job, an often-burdensome process. Organizations can encourage employees to make changes by measuring business and employee performance with metrics that evaluate consumer relationships and adjust compensation structures accordingly. How are employees evaluated today, and do those criteria encourage consumer-centric behaviors? How are the organization's and the employees' performances evaluated, and are those evaluations in line with consumer centricity?

Leveraging Digital to Transform

"There's not a single player in the industry that's going to re-innovate healthcare. The growth opportunity is going to come from other companies, and this growth opportunity is going to be massive."
—Jeff Dachis, CEO, One Drop

We started this book talking about the rise of the e-consumer, the person who demands more from healthcare, who expects to be empowered, engaged, equipped and enabled in the management of his or her own care. Healthcare organizations have a big task learning to handle this consumer; and while they are trying to become consumer-centric, smaller and more nimble competitors are diving into their markets. Those small companies are quickly building capabilities that are potentially disruptive.

That's why we recommend that traditional healthcare organizations look for smart alliances with digital companies to accelerate their shift to consumer centricity. Of course, building digital alliances and partnerships is not the only option. We've seen organizations like Geisinger Health build digital capabilities internally, for example. But partnerships are often the fastest approach, given the cultural barriers and legacy systems that stand in the way of digital transformation.

THE BARRIERS TO DIGITAL AT TRADITIONAL HEALTHCARE ORGANIZATIONS

Most traditional healthcare organizations were founded well before the information age and face many obstacles to implementing innovation and digital. Adopting and scaling a new capability, like digital into a legacy system, will require more significant investment in new architectures and talent acquisition. "The infrastructure changes are a huge burden on the system. We were not built, from the get-go, with a consumer-first orientation. It is much harder to change a legacy operating system when you're not building from the ground up," says George Sauter, Chief Strategy Officer at John Muir Health.

We spoke with one healthcare leader who runs a data-collection startup, and he tells us that even though his platform is fully HIPAA-compliant and secure, one of his largest insurance clients took two-and-a-half years to approve the cloud-based technology. In addition to clunky legacy systems, traditional organizations have a cultural orientation to the status quo that is risk averse and hinders digital integration altogether. When Prophet worked with a large multinational pharmaceutical company that was trying to become more consumer-centric, the biggest barrier was cultural hesitation. There was neither a willingness to take on the financial investment in becoming more digital nor was there the drive to take on the structural investments associated with change.

When we surveyed healthcare leaders, less than 10 percent reported an interest in working with a partner in digital health. Payer and pharma companies prefer to partner with providers, and providers would rather partner with payers. That is likely due to the cultural barriers and hesitations regarding the longevity and stability of newer companies. However, organizations have a great opportunity to take advantage of the capabilities and products of those newer companies by working with them to accelerate the consumer-centric transformation. "You have to keep an open mind about what is out there and what solutions capabilities exist," says Tom Feitel, Global Head of Enterprise Customer Solutions at Medocity, Inc. "Sometimes it helps to get out of an 'invented-here' mindset."

Unlike the long processes associated with M&A or internal capability building, digital health partnerships can enable traditional organizations to quickly acquire digital capabilities and talent and also gain exposure to innovative, agile and consumer-centric mindsets and cultures. Partnering with a digital health company can also offset the procedural barriers to delivering more engaging experiences. And partnering can inspire leadership to merge the expertise of traditional healthcare with the expertise of digitally enabled consumer-facing companies. "We bring the consumer-facing capabilities from a digital perspective, and they bring the clinical know-how. Working together allows new ideas to flourish," says Kevin Kumler, President of Health Systems at Zocdoc. Even at a tactical level, partnerships can add new perspective. When Zocdoc partners with major hospitals, it often introduces the Net Promoter Score (NPS) as a key measurement of success. That metric, widely used in other categories, emphasizes relationship building, which can lead organizations to look at the experience holistically.

Partnership also works in favor of digital health companies; even though those companies have the agility and expertise to make offerings that are more relevant to the e-consumer, they lack the trusting relationships that many traditional healthcare organizations have with consumers. Digital health companies are relentlessly looking for opportunities to demonstrate value to investors, widen their apertures and expand their platforms beyond their initial audience. A partnership with an established healthcare organization helps introduce small companies to a large consumer base while also expanding the organization's overall consumer-centric reputation. It's a win-win.

PARTNERING FOR CONSUMER-CENTRIC EXPERIENCES: FIVE KEY COMPONENTS

Given the mutually beneficial nature of digital health partnerships, traditional organizations should explore the gaps in the consumer experience and evaluate where they can most effectively use outside digital capabilities. To help traditional organizations better serve their consumers, we believe digital health companies can pull five key levers: content, user interface, community, data and platform.

Experience Components of a Digital Partnership

BENEFITS CONSUMERS SEE			BENEFITS ORGANIZATIONS SEE	
Content	User Interface	Community	Data	Platform

The five levers are present both internally and externally. Content, interface and community are all benefits that the consumer experiences. The consumer will interact with the content, engage with the interface and participate in the community. At the same time, data and platform—which happen behind the scenes—provide additional value that consumers may not see.

FOCUS ON BENEFITS THAT CONSUMERS SEE

Content engages consumers with relevant information, real-time and usually on-demand. It may include images, videos, notifications or tutorials. It is important, given how inundated consumers are with information from various organizations, that relevant content grabs the consumer's attention and provides value. User interface involves user-friendly platforms and experiences that meet the same standards of consumer-facing brands like Sephora, Facebook or Amazon. In addition to content and user interface, which are more tactile parts of the experience, digital health companies are masters at fostering community. Communities can bring together patients, doctors and experts.

FIND INTEGRATIONS THAT POWER THE EXPERIENCE

Because digital health companies can build content, interface and communities that encourage and promote consumer engagement; they can also gather data that healthcare organizations can't. Take for example AIA's partnership with Vitality, the science backed wellness proposition. Without AIA Vitality's interactive and engaging interface and content, AIA wouldn't be able to track the daily wellness data for its members. Now, AIA can use this information to deliver improved value and better enhance its relationship with consumers. Now, AIA can use that information to better enhance the relationship with its consumers. In addition, digital health companies build platforms of systems, integrations and processes that form the foundation for a new consumer-centric experience. Digital data-collection companies like Tonic Health, which we will explore later, or Flatiron Health can integrate their data with the EMR data in health systems with little to no disruption. "We recognize the position these organizations are in and their need to also use hospital systems like EPIC and Cerner, so part of our job is making it easy to integrate with these systems and also help them interface with separate data sources that exist within their own organization," says Julia Morton, Flatiron's Senior Director, Customer Success.

By more effectively leveraging partnerships to close experience gaps, traditional healthcare organizations can focus on driving deeper consideration, preference and loyalty. Now, let's look at examples of how organizations can capitalize on the five levers of digital health.

CREATE CONTENT THAT ENGAGES

Content is a critical component of any great consumer experience. From Sephora's Pinterest-like Beauty Board to The Skimm's daily news updates, consumers engage most with brands that serve up important content in interesting, new ways. Content that is personalized and timely helps create a seamless and cohesive experience. Organizations that deliver relevant content to serve specific consumer needs not only see impressive engagement levels but also create a powerful platform for growth.

Traditional healthcare organizations are not known for pushing digestible and consumer-friendly content. They instead rely on clipboards for collecting inpatient data, pamphlets for public health information and snail mail for important updates on bill payments or doctor visits. When organizations use methods like those, they collect suboptimal data and often fail to effectively convey their message. Most importantly, they miss the opportunity to get consumers to act. More engaging content benefits consumers but also helps the organization collect more user data, creating a virtual engagement loop. Of course, traditional companies can create relevant content on their own—but digital companies can do it faster.

Emmi Solutions Engages Consumers at University Hospitals

Traditional organizations typically lean on their agencies and internal content teams to generate consumer content, but many have an opportunity to tap into the interactive content created by digital health companies. In 2014, University Hospitals—a leading healthcare system based in Cleveland, Ohio—entered into a long-term partnership with Emmi Solutions to help drive a more engaging consumer experience.[55] Emmi Solutions' personalized technology platform provides compelling, interactive and easily digestible content that engages patients, drives adherence and increases patient satisfaction. The partnership gives University Hospitals access to the robust arsenal of consumer-centric content, which includes anything from tips for visiting the doctor's office and interactive explanations of diagnoses to personalized walk-throughs of treatment experiences. Through consistent evaluation and optimization, Emmi offers University Hospitals quality content that will update and evolve to meet changing consumer needs. The increased engagement that has come from the Emmi partnership has produced higher patient-satisfaction scores and increased adherence to treatment plans. "Our expanded relationship with University Hospitals will have significance beyond the benefits gained from implementation," says Emmi Solutions CEO Devin Gross in his company's press release.[56] "Due to the time span, we'll be able to more fully understand and refine our solutions' capabilities, ushering in a new era of patient engagement at a critically sensitive time for an industry in flux."

MAKE INTERFACES INVITING, NOT BORING

With the rise of design-centered technologies, consumers are increasingly demanding clean, easily navigable, modern user

---

55   https://www.emmisolutions.com/news/university-hospitals-and-emmi-solutions-partner-on-commitment-to-patient-engagement/

56   https://www.emmisolutions.com/news/university-hospitals-and-emmi-solutions-partner-on-commitment-to-patient-engagement/

interfaces. Long gone are the days when organizations could get away with clunky, monochromatic, text-heavy websites. Today, consumers expect user interfaces that are intuitive, visually appealing and optimized to engage even on the smallest devices, like a smartphone or wearable. Yet healthcare organizations have a reputation for dated user interfaces. (Epic's MyChart, for example, is reminiscent of websites from the 1990s). Those user interfaces don't attract consumers or encourage engagement. Partnerships with digital companies would help.

Tonic Health, the Interactive Patient Data-Collection System

Health systems have traditionally leveraged inefficient and cumbersome data-collection methods, such as filling out clipboards in the waiting room. Tonic Health is a digital data-collection platform that helps solve that issue. The cloud-based platform allows healthcare organizations to collect the right information from the right patient on the right device in the right setting at the right time—and seamlessly combines it all on the backend to provide one unified view of the patient or patient population. Tonic's fully customizable survey platform provides a Disney-like experience with gamification and animation elements at key touchpoints along a patient's care journey, including patient intake and registration, payments, consent forms, health-risk assessments and screeners, advance care planning and more. "Tonic captures and communicates the patient voice. Tonic does for healthcare what mobility did for airline check-in: make it seamless, easy and intuitive for patients to fill out any survey or form and make any payment from any device. No more paper forms, no more paper bills, no more boring clipboards asking for the same information. The result is a win-win. Patients enjoy a great experience, and providers enjoy significant cost reduction," says CEO Sterling Lanier. Tonic partners with health systems and produces richer and more helpful data. And importantly, its valuable services provide a halo effect to the outdated healthcare system.

Tonic Health partnered with MedStar, the largest provider in the Washington, D.C. metro, to enhance data collection. The platform improved the experience of both the consumer and the staff. Additionally, the data from the platform revealed that Med Star could fit 2.5 appointments in an hour versus 2. That discovery increased the system's revenue potential by 25 percent. Further, the data gathered with Tonic leads to more personalized experiences. One physician at UCLA says that Tonic revolutionized data collection in ways that improved her in-person interactions with patients. Thanks to the platform, she knows how to engage with the patient in a "hyper-personal" way.

FOSTERING COMMUNITY AND FACILITATING DIALOGUE

One of the biggest challenges with new consumer experiences is driving adoption—or, in the case of healthcare, driving treatment plan adherence. Fostering a broad community, curated for individual users with specific conditions or needs, can help engage consumers. It can also generate several benefits for the business by revealing specific consumer insights, potentially generating low-cost content and adding a personal element to an experience that keeps users coming back.

Vibrant, online communities can make consumers feel better informed, empowering them to learn from their peers in safe environments. The communities allow consumers to bypass WebMD and talk to patients like themselves. Online communities also allow patients to engage in one-on-one conversations with experts. As a result, an environment of transparency and collaboration materializes between consumers and healthcare organizations. In the healthcare industry, an established social community isn't just a consumer social network. Rather, it can truly be a powerful motivator to keep consumers engaged during their healthcare journey.

Shire + PatientsLikeMe Let Patient Voices Be Heard

Shire, the largest rare-disease biotech company, partnered with PatientsLikeMe to get a more complete picture of the patient and caregiver experience. When working with Shire, PatientsLikeMe focused on rare-disease states that typically don't have large communities. "When the disease is severe enough, socially isolating enough or has a long road to diagnosis, then patients can really benefit from the shared learnings and social connectedness of the community. The more the patient knows that what they're feeling matters throughout the course of diagnosis and treatment, the better off we are," says Brad Gescheider, Senior Director of Strategic Partnerships and Care Solutions.

The PatientsLikeMe partnership also bolsters Shire's understanding of outcomes and treatment experiences. By using PatientsLikeMe to study a specific group of patients—rather than limiting data to clinical-trials information—Shire was able to reach a wider number of patients with highly specialized conditions. The partnership with PatientsLikeMe improved awareness and education around rare diseases and informed Shire's approaches for improving outcomes.

COLLECTING DATA THAT LEADS TO ENGAGEMENT

The most engaging companies can leverage and analyze a broad array of data sets and sources to provide real-time, personalized experiences. The data that healthcare organizations use today focuses on clinical trials, treatment outcomes and claims data. Healthcare organizations have the potential, however, to harness an enormous amount of data regarding consumer needs, preferences, attitudes, behaviors and motivations. Those additional data points can inform consumer preferences, satisfaction and other metrics to drive experience improvements. But, because the organizations often don't use that additional data, healthcare organizations are inclined to deliver sub-par experiences and are unable to deliver the right experience to consumers at the right time. Digital companies can help.

Pfizer and IBM Watson Health Redefine Cancer Treatment

IBM's Watson is perhaps the most well-known mechanism for aggregating and analyzing massive amounts of data. IBM Watson Health partnered with pharmaceutical giant Pfizer to define new treatments for cancer by linking unstructured clinical data with additional information regarding medical expertise, patient lifestyles, interests and other factors that influence cancer treatment. The partnership allows Pfizer to unlock the value of consumer data that could reveal important insights about designing personalized treatment.[57] While Watson Health's solutions are best known for their implications for clinical care, the program's ability to integrate clinical and nonclinical data about consumers has the potential to impact the patient experience. "Watson's ability to learn and adapt for clinical purposes is unique, and I think the possibilities for the broader experience are just as significant," says Dusty Majumdar, former Chief Marketing Officer at Watson Health. "It's not just about making the most accurate diagnosis or designing the best treatment plan; it's about enabling organizations to create more relevant consumer experiences and ones that produce the best outcome possible."

---

57   https://www.forbes.com/sites/brucejapsen/2016/12/01/pfizer-partners-with-ibm-watson-to-advance-cancer-drug-discovery/#455580791b1e

DEVELOP A WINNING PLATFORM

Seamless and cohesive experiences are often built on top of a comprehensive, unified information and data platform. A great platform makes it easy to connect all the touchpoints of the consumer experience and allows for the addition and incorporation of new and relevant functionalities. When digital platforms were introduced into the healthcare space, the focus was on helping systems become more efficient. The creation of EMR systems, which often lack interoperability, may have led to greater efficiency within a single system but also hindered the ability to create remarkable consumer experiences throughout the ecosystem. "Many of those systems focus on the needs of the provider," says Lee Shapiro, digital healthcare entrepreneur and board member of Livongo, "but aren't always built with the patient experience in mind." Platforms like MyChart, Epic and Allscripts are really meant to enhance the work of the provider, not the patient. Digital health partnerships can provide a way for large healthcare organizations to quickly build and activate seamless consumer experiences.

Zocdoc Creates a Platform for Both Providers and Consumers

Since its founding in 2017, U.S.-based Zocdoc has built a robust platform with the goal of making healthcare interactions easier and more accessible for patients. Zocdoc's platform integrates with EHRs to revolutionize the way patients make their doctor appointments. The platform makes searching for a doctor, confirming insurance, scheduling an appointment and filling out pre-visit forms as simple as making reservations at a restaurant. Although originally focused on private practices, Zocdoc now has partnerships with major hospital networks like NYU Langone Medical Center. Typically, those providers already have scheduling capabilities through their EHR systems; since 2016, however, Zocdoc can integrate with

EHR systems and improve the experience for consumers. "Zocdoc's innovative work has helped to optimize our appointment inventory and enhance our patients' access to care," says Nader Mherabi, Senior Vice President and Vice Dean, Chief Information Officer, at NYU Langone Medical Center, in a Zocdoc press release.[58] "We are excited about their new integration, which will empower a more seamless experience."

In addition to providing a more patient-centric appointment experience, Zocdoc helps hospitals operate at full capacity. "When we talk to health systems about improving access for patients, they tell us that there just aren't appointments available," says Jeff Yuan, General Manager of Health Systems. "When we look at the data, they are right. Many providers are booked days or weeks in advance. But when you look backwards, the average health system is filling only around two-thirds of inventory due to last-minute cancellations or appointment rescheduling—all while consumers are precisely looking for near-term availability." In addition to its scheduling functionality, the Zocdoc platform enables real-time feedback by allowing patients to rate an experience; it also lets patients "check in" in advance of appointments in order to reduce waiting time.

LEARN FROM CLEVELAND CLINIC: OSCAR HELPS FIND NEW PATIENTS

While not all digital health partnerships will provide all five key components of the consumer-centric experience, most will cover at least a few. The partnership between Cleveland Clinic and Oscar Health is a good example. After the enactment of the Affordable Care Act, Cleveland Clinic needed to quickly create a way to serve

---

58   https://www.zocdoc.com/about/news/zocdoc-announces-new-ehr-integration-improve-access-interoperability-health-systems-patients/

patients with individual insurance plans while upholding its high standard of patient satisfaction. The solution for Cleveland Clinic was a partnership with digital health insurance company Oscar Health. Oscar's primary product targets consumers in the individual market. In 2018, Oscar Health partnered with Cleveland Clinic to deliver co-branded health insurance plans to Cleveland residents. The plans, which are the Clinic's first foray into the insurance business, give members access to Cleveland Clinic's world-renowned network of doctors and specialists combined with Oscar's full suite of benefits, including a personalized concierge team, free 24/7 Doctor on Call and a seamless app experience.

Unlike other large traditional payers, Oscar's content and interface resemble that of a technology company more than an insurance provider. Oscar provides a personal concierge team, a database of patient history and care needs, telehealth integrations and a personalized companion app that logs and tracks every interaction. The app's content provides an engaging way for members to report symptoms and find physicians.

A Common Integrated Platform and Data

The partnership between Cleveland Clinic and Oscar Health offers a unique, individualized healthcare plan for patients in specific areas of Ohio. Patients can sign up themselves and their families for a plan that resembles familiar policies, with co-pays and deductibles, but also includes Oscar's unique platform features. The partnership provides a seamless connection between the provider and the payer through Oscar's telemedicine platform and through the integration of referrals from primary-care physicians and specialists and appointment booking. The partnership also enables the flow of patient information. All treatment information logged through Cleveland Clinic's EMR system is funneled back to Oscar, breaking down the walls that typically prevent providers and payers from communicating.

From a business standpoint, both parties see major advantages. In addition to helping each other grow, the biggest advantage comes from simplifying the payer-provider information exchange. Oscar can grow its consumer base through the broader exposure to Cleveland Clinic patients and by offering better care than any other individual plan. In addition, the partnership lets Oscar know, in real-time, where the patient is receiving care. From its side of the partnership, Cleveland Clinic can take advantage of the Oscar platform to simplify its connections with the patients, monitor adherence and avoid unnecessary visits. The venture helps both parties minimize the back and forth that often occurs when providers and payers operate independently and also helps to connect the ecosystem for consumers. "Many people don't know where to start looking for care; and once they go to someone, there are no clear next steps," says Eddie Segel, Senior Vice President of Business at Oscar. "The data isn't shared between healthcare silos. They bounce around the system. This causes bad experiences and accrues unnecessary care costs and causes patient frustration and dissatisfaction." In February 2018, the Oscar-Cleveland Clinic healthcare plan captured an estimated 15 percent of the individual market in the 2018 open-enrollment season, nearly 40 percent more than expected, according to Kevin Sears, Executive Director of Cleveland Clinic Market & Network Services.[59]

FINDING YOUR PERFECT DIGITAL PARTNER

Despite the preference of traditional organizations to partner with each other, our survey showed that only one in five of those organizations are completely unwilling to partner with innovative

---

[59] http://www.modernhealthcare.com/article/20180205/NEWS/180209954

companies—suggesting that, when it comes to digital partnerships, the issue is not unwillingness but, rather, know-how. Creating strong, mutually beneficial partnerships with healthcare startups does not happen overnight. The best partnerships are formed with clear business goals in mind and a path for execution. When considering partnerships with digital companies, organizations can take these steps:

Considerations in Forming a Digital Partnership	
Step 1	Identify and Assess Gaps
Step 2	Map the Landscape
Step 3	Outline the Terms of the Partnership
Step 4	Don't Fund, Co-Create

Step 1: Identify and Assess Gaps

First, organizations should identify and assess gaps in the consumer experience and then select the areas where the right digital partnership will drive the most impact and value. Then, the organization can assess current initiatives with a critical eye and define where a digital partnership is a better option than buying resources or building in-house capabilities. If a digital partnership is the best option, organizations should establish a clear vision of how it will improve the consumer experience.

Step 2: Map the Landscape

Next, healthcare organizations can map the landscape to narrow the field of potential digital partners based on business priorities. Countless healthcare startups address similar needs, so the organization must search for companies that are a good fit based on capability and culture. The organization can then build a set of prioritized criteria to narrow down the list of partnerships to pursue. Prioritization also gives the organization an understanding of the landscape of potential competitors.

Step 3: Outline the Terms of the Partnership

Once a partner has been identified, the healthcare organization will need to define a clear partnership value exchange in order to start the conversation. Defining a win-win value exchange is often where healthcare partnerships go awry, because there is no clear understanding of what each party gains from the other. Healthcare startups always benefit from the institutional knowledge and scale of the large healthcare organizations. It is the responsibility of digital health companies to articulate what they can offer, how they can fill gaps and how they align with the business goals of the traditional healthcare organization.

Step 4: Don't Fund, Co-Create

Finally, healthcare organizations should keep in mind that collaboration is key. Traditional healthcare organizations should start partnerships with co-creation sessions (see the Fourth Shift), setting the precedent that the partnership will be one of collaboration, not investment. The sessions are opportunities to float new ideas and brainstorm how those ideas can be improved. The sessions are opportunities to set up teams and workshops that will continue to drive new solutions as the partnership evolves.

As healthcare organizations explore the possibilities of partnering with digital health companies, they will begin to realize the consumer experience and engagement growth potential. For many years, healthcare organizations have relied on internal forces to drive change and engage consumers; but the opportunity for partnering with a digital health company is not one that healthcare organizations should pass up. Leveraging the respective strengths of both traditional healthcare organizations and digital health companies will produce more engaging consumer experiences and help drive the organization's orientation toward a more consumer-centric future. It's a win-win proposition.

Conclusion

The Path to Transformation

I n *Making the Healthcare Shift*, we have explored five critical shifts that organizations need to embrace in order to address the ever-changing needs of the e-consumer and win in the increasingly competitive healthcare markets. Let's quickly review:

THE FIRST SHIFT: From Tactical Fixes to a Holistic Experience Strategy

Healthcare organizations often begin to enhance the consumer experience in one-off initiatives, like reducing wait times or filling out online forms. Developing a comprehensive and unifying consumer-centric strategy, however, can strategically shift the organization to more successfully win the hearts and minds of consumers.

THE SECOND SHIFT: From Fragmented Care to Connected Ecosystems

Although payers, providers and pharma companies are finding new ways to work together, the healthcare journey remains fragmented, causing frustration and inefficiency. When healthcare organizations operate in a connected ecosystem, rather than as standalone entities, they can better engage consumers in meaningful ways. And that makes both the consumer and the enterprise healthier.

THE THIRD SHIFT: From Population-Centric to Person-Centered

Organizations often focus on creating products, services and experiences for groups of similar consumers, such as those who have the same condition or those who fall into the same demographic. But no two consumers are exactly alike. To be truly consumer-centric, it is important to engage consumers in hyper-personalized ways in order to meet their unique, individual needs.

THE FOURTH SHIFT: From Incremental Improvements to Pervasive Innovation

Today, organizations tackle small and time-consuming improvements to established systems and processes that were not designed with the consumer in mind. To put the focus on the consumer, organizations must reimagine their approach to innovation. By adopting a minimally viable product mindset or consulting external sources for innovation inspiration, an organization can fundamentally change its approach to innovation and accomplish meaningful and consistent streams of product, service and experience enhancements.

THE FIFTH SHIFT: From Insights as a Department to a Culture of Consumer Obsession

Establishing insights as a function is critical to gathering intelligence, but it's not enough. Healthcare organizations can go further by creating a culture of consumer obsession, where everyone in the organization always keeps the consumer front and center.

We also explored two critical enablers that will maximize any organization's efforts toward making a successful healthcare shift. These include:

Cultural Transformation

As organizations make the shift to consumer centricity, they will need the full support of a culture that recognizes and respects the value of the consumer in everything that they do. Bringing employees along on the journey and equipping them to help the organization win is critical to success.

Digital Transformation

As organizations work to execute a consumer-centric strategy, they need to embrace digital disruption as an opportunity for growth and an accelerator for change. By keeping an open mind toward smart digital alliances and partnerships, organizations can jump-start their journey to consumer centricity and improved outcomes.

Together, the five shifts—along with cultural transformation and digital transformation—can help healthcare organizations meet and exceed the needs of today's e-consumers. The five shifts, however, are not sequential; the path and order in which an organization pursues them depends entirely on the needs of the organization and the role of the individuals leading the charge. To conclude our examination of the shift to consumer centricity, we will outline a few different paths that leaders can take to jump-start their efforts—recognizing, of course, that change may emanate from anywhere in the organization.

EXECUTIVE LED: TOP DOWN TRANSFORMATION

C-Suite executives are in a unique position to accelerate the journey to consumer centricity. With an initial focus on the First Shift, they can uniquely jump-start the journey by defining what it should look like at their organization and by role-modeling consumer-obsessed behaviors. As we discussed, however, committing to consumer centricity requires more than words; it requires action. We saw how Dr. David Feinberg shifted Geisinger Health's direction toward consumer centricity when he joined the organization. "He made a clear case for focusing on the patient experience as a primary target and for focusing overall on a brand that we have called 'Caring' that represented how we set up a healthcare ecosystem in which you step into a hospital and don't even realize you're in the hospital," says Geisinger CIO Alistair Erskine, M.D. Dr. Feinberg knew that focus would be impactful only if he brought it to life, which led to Geisinger's ProvenExperience refund program.

In addition to having the power to steer the strategic direction of the organization, executives have enormous influence in setting the stage for a consumer-obsessed culture. In the chapter "Creating a Consumer-Centric Culture," we learned that the strongest changes begin at the very top of the organization and travel down. That requires executives to articulate their vision in ways that are accessible to employees and to model behaviors that support consumer obsession. Novant Health CEO Carl Armato did that when he orchestrated the creation of the People's Credo, which outlines the ways employees should treat each other, and the Standards of Service, which outlines the ways employees should treat consumers. Setting a standard for both the consumer and the employee experience led to what Armato calls "the human experience." Executive support of initiatives like that accelerates the adoption of consumer centricity.

Once a direction for consumer centricity has been determined, executives can focus on bringing everyone's voice into the conversation. "To be inclusive is to accept, encourage and respect different perspectives. We've always been collaborative but have worked hard to evolve our culture so we're not so 'top down.' We make sure that everyone has a seat at the table, including when we design our products," says Andrew Dreyfus, CEO of BCBSMA. "In addition to being the right thing to do, it's a business imperative—because being diverse and inclusive provides a competitive advantage and allows us to truly meet the needs of our customers." For BCBSMA, that meant building a leadership team with diverse backgrounds, geographies and perspectives that was a closer representation of the members that the organization serves.

Beyond the large-scale, more official moves, executives should be cognizant of their position as role models and demonstrate ways to weave consumer centricity into the organization. Indiana University Health's CEO Dennis Murphy thinks about this role all the time and commits small acts to set a big precedent for his teams. He sends handwritten notes and certificates to employees receiving awards for consumer-centric behaviors to demonstrate, in a very personal way, leadership's recognition of and appreciation for the work. Murphy also makes rounds on hospital floors to talk with patients who have the fewest visitors. "I make sure those people get a chance to talk to somebody. I go into the patient's room, get them water and help them feel personally supported. It sets an example that you don't fully appreciate until you leave the floor and somebody tells you that the staff was blown away that you talked with that specific patient," says Murphy. Executives may have the highest positions in the organization; but when it comes to making the biggest impression on culture, they are often most impactful at the ground level.

After executives have set the strategic vision and laid the foundation for a consumer-obsessed culture, they can begin to use the support and expertise of others. They can start working with their fellow leaders to ignite change across the organization. They can work with the chief marketing officer to bolster insights or collaborate with business-unit leaders to infuse innovation into the organization's DNA.

MARKETING LED: BRINGING FUNCTIONAL CHANGE

As the function typically responsible for knowing consumers best, marketing often plays a key role in transformation. Some marketing leaders have a seat next to the executive leaders and can take the approach outlined for executive leaders. That is what happened for Matt Gove, Chief Consumer Officer at Piedmont Healthcare. Working closely with CEO Kevin Brown, Gove drove alignment regarding what consumer centricity would look like at the health system, developed a roadmap of moves and then implemented appropriate programs such as same-day scheduling and physician ratings and reviews. Gove's situation is typical at most healthcare organizations. Many marketing leaders, however, do not have the influence to spark wide-scale change. Those who are still strengthening their teams and building organizational authority need to take another approach and focus their initial efforts on the Fifth Shift, turning consumer insights into—as Scott Davis explains in his 2009 book *The Shift: The Transformation of Today's Marketers Into Tomorrow's Growth Leaders*—a secret weapon.

Focusing on the Fifth Shift will help leaders establish a stronger insights capability and uncover the insights that will lead to action. That is what Stacey Geffken at Geisinger Health Plan did when she transformed a small function of market researchers who occasionally conducted focus groups into a high-functioning team that regularly collects and analyzes consumer data to find the most relevant insights. Aetna's Dave Edelman acted similarly, bolstering the enterprise intelligence function by consolidating marketing, branding and insights under his leadership. By bringing those previously siloed functions together, he built the foundation for a consumer understanding that would eventually lead to developing ways to deepen engagement and experience, both internally and externally. "Our early quick wins came in the form of helping our sales teams take greater advantage of digital channels and bring the power of smarter analytics into their go-to-market strategies. That led to some immediate wins and established our credibility," says Edelman.

Once marketing leaders have developed the organizational foundation for consumer insight development, they can move to the Third Shift to apply those insights for greater consumer personalization and even greater impact. That is what David Duvall did at Novant Health when he led the charge on market segmentation, an effort that fueled the creation of content and programs better targeted to the system's unique consumers. Marketing can also play a key role in establishing any external partnerships that may enhance the organization's ability to create personalized experiences. We saw this with organizations like MedStar Health and Shire, which use digital partnerships with companies like Tonic Health and PatientsLikeMe that enhance and accelerate the personalization of services.

As insights begin to flow through the organization to inform key decisions, marketing begins to influence innovation efforts in the way that Kelly Jo Golson did at Advocate Health Care. In that effort, marketing leaders will likely face skepticism from leadership; but they must be persistent in showing impact. "You fight the hesitation by innovating in small ways and proving yourself. You fight it by proving a positive ROI and always bringing the consumer voice to the table," says Margaret Coughlin, former Chief Marketing Officer of Mount Sinai Health as of early 2018.

To recap, marketing is typically viewed as the team that understands the consumer best; so making inroads in the Third and Fifth Shift should be the focus. Those leaders should consistently use the consumer's voice to win over leadership. That will not only establish credibility for the marketing team but will also be integral to the broader organization's ability to make progress. Katie Logan, Piedmont's Vice President of Experience, sums it up best: "We have to make the consumer voice an active part of the conversation and ensure that we operate not according to what we *think* people want but what people are actually telling us they want."

BUILDING A MOVEMENT FROM THE GROUND UP

Executive leadership and marketing leaders are not the only ones who can push consumer centricity. Leaders across other functions—such as operations, customer service, digital or IT—may not have the influence of executive leadership or marketing, but they can play a critical role in igniting change. They may not have the power to mandate the creation of an insights team or a segmentation analysis, but they can identify consumer pain points in their purview and work closely with the research team to determine what insights are currently available. That is the role played by Matthias Krebs at Novant Health, when he worked one-on-one with other functions to help solve their unique business challenges with insights. At first, Krebs' influence was small; however, the word spread as he continued to demonstrate impact, and demand for insight-driven decision-making grew. Some leaders will conduct their own research on a small, targeted scale. Consider Amgen's STATWISE™ program for rheumatoid arthritis, which we discussed in the Fifth Shift. To arrive at the insight that led to the text-based adherence program, the team conducted focus groups with rheumatoid arthritis patients. They didn't run a full-scale market analysis. They remained focused on their area of influence to arrive at an insight that was relevant to patients.

Transformation may occur faster from the executive boardrooms, but it certainly doesn't have to begin there. If other business leaders work from the ground up and gain advocates along the way, they, too, can ignite change by diligently connecting everything they do back to the consumer and ensuring that their efforts ladder up to the greater strategy. Katie Logan certainly found that to be true when introducing consumer-centric initiatives to specialty clinics across the Piedmont system—initiatives such as online scheduling that would disrupt the way the clinics were accustomed to working. "We have to link it back to the strategy, help the organization understand the why and see the value propositions for them and the patients," she says.

THE FUTURE OF CONSUMER CENTRICITY

For any of the five shifts or enablers to take hold, time, investment and patience is required regardless of whether the move is a wholesale transformation or a step toward change in an on-going journey. There will be hiccups along the way. But as the organization moves forward, it will begin to see results. Beyond improved business outcomes, organizations will enjoy the impact that consumer centricity can have on the patients they serve. From the Mount Sinai patient who can recover in the comfort of his own home—because he is better informed about his procedure and has financial support for physical therapy—to the National Health Service COPD patient who can now easily track her progress with digital tools, consumers are developing new relationships with organizations that promote health across the entire journey. Patients are empowered to collaborate with healthcare organizations and their established ecosystems to more effectively manage their own health and live better lives. Consumer centricity makes it all possible and more probable. Consumer centricity is the solution that will allow the healthcare businesses to grow, the consumers they care for to thrive and the communities they live in to flourish.

About the Authors

Scott M. Davis:

Scott is the Chief Growth Officer of Prophet, a leading strategic growth firm. In over 25 years of brand and marketing strategy consulting, he has worked across an array of clients, including, GE, Allstate, Hershey's, Microsoft, Boeing, Sara Lee, NBC Universal, the NBA, Target, Gulfstream, United Airlines, the City of Chicago.  His work in healthcare includes Johnson & Johnson, the Blue Cross Blue Shield Association, Mayo Clinic, Novant Health and an array of provider systems in the US and across the globe. Scott is a frequent guest lecturer at MBA programs across the country and served as an adjunct professor at the Kellogg School of Management at Northwestern University. Scott began his career at Procter & Gamble. Scott is a contributing columnist at forbes.com, and is the author of 3 previous books, including *The Shift: The Transformation of Today's Marketers into Tomorrow's Growth Leaders*.

Jeff Gourdji:

Jeff is a Partner and co-leader of the healthcare practice at Prophet. With over 20 years of leading high-impact marketing & strategy projects, Jeff brings a breadth of experience that comes from working across many industries as marketing practitioner, management consultant and political strategist. Jeff has worked extensively across the healthcare value chain across an array of growth challenges. His current and past clients include Mayo Clinic, Northwestern Medicine, Encompass Health, Anthem, Eli Lilly & Company and several Blue Cross Blue Shield plans. Jeff is a frequent speaker and writer on healthcare topics, and has been published or cited in Becker's Hospital Review, Modern Healthcare, Medical Marketing & Media (MM&M), PM 360 and MediaPost. Jeff received his B.A. from the University of Michigan and his M.B.A. from the University of Chicago Booth School of Business.

Appendix

THE STATE OF CONSUMER-CENTRICITY IN HEALTHCARE

To understand where healthcare organizations stand in making the shifts described in this book, to understand where they have made progress, and where they have struggled, we surveyed 241 healthcare executives (VP level or higher in provider and payer organizations, Sr Director or above in pharmaceutical manufacturing organizations) in late 2017. While findings have been interspersed through the pages, additional data can be found here, including cuts by type of healthcare organization and by region.

Reported Progress on Each Shift

BOLD   HIGH
UNDERLINED   MEDIUM
ITALIZIZED   LOW

	TOTAL	U.S.	U.K.	Germany	China	Japan	Provider	Payer	Pharma
	X	A	B	C	D	E	F	G	H
BASE	241.0	146.0	30*	30*	25**	10**	105.0	40*	96*
Experience Strategy	*6%*	*6%*	–	17%	*4%*	–	*8%*	–	*6%*
Connected Ecosystems	*9%*	*10%*	–	13%	*4%*	**20%**	*8%*	*8%*	12%
Person-Centered	12%	*9%*	**20%**	**27%**	*4%*	**20%**	*9%*	*3%*	**21%**
Pervasive Innovation	12%	*9%*	**20%**	13%	12%	**30%**	14%	–	15%
Culture of Consumer Obsession	15%	14%	*10%*	**23%**	16%	**20%**	14%	15%	16%

P1A-P5A: Where your organization is today - Bottom 2 Box* Summary (N=241)
*Note: Bottom 2 Box represents the *highest* level of progress on each shift

Source: 2017 Prophet Healthcare Consumerism Study
Respondents are healthcare executives across the globe

Reported Progress on Shift 1

BOLD   HIGH
UNDERLINED   MEDIUM
ITALISIZED   LOW

	TOTAL	U.S.	U.K.	Germany	China	Japan	Provider	Payer	Pharma
	X	A	B	C	D	E	F	G	H
BASE	241.0	146.0	30*	30*	25**	10**	105.0	40*	96*
Top 2 Box (Net) (Tactical Fixes)	47%	*41%*	**53%**	**53%**	**60%**	50%	43%	**60%**	45%
Bottom 2 Box (Net) (Experience Strategy)	6%	6%	–	17%	4%	–	8%	–	6%

Q: Where your organization is today - FROM: Tactical Fixes (7), TO: Experience Strategy (1) (N=241)

Source: 2017 Prophet Healthcare Consumerism Study
Respondents are healthcare executives across the globe

Reported Progress on Shift 2

BOLD HIGH
UNDERLINED MEDIUM
ITALIZED LOW

	TOTAL	U.S.	U.K.	Germany	China	Japan	Provider	Payer	Pharma
	X	A	B	C	D	E	F	G	H
BASE	241.0	146.0	30*	30*	25**	10**	105.0	40*	96*
Top 2 Box (Net) (Fragmented Care Acts)	41%	37%	53%	30%	68%	30%	38%	68%	33%
Bottom 2 Box (Net) (Connected Ecosystems)	9%	10%	–	13%	4%	20%	8%	8%	12%

Q: Where your organization is today - FROM: Fragmented Care Acts (7), TO: Connected Ecosystems (1) (N=241)

Source: 2017 Prophet Healthcare Consumerism Study
Respondents are healthcare executives across the globe

Reported Progress on Shift 3

BOLD HIGH
UNDERLINED MEDIUM
ITALIZED LOW

	TOTAL	U.S.	U.K.	Germany	China	Japan	Provider	Payer	Pharma
	X	A	B	C	D	E	F	G	H
BASE	241.0	146.0	30*	30*	25**	10**	105.0	40*	96*
Top 2 Box (Net) (Population-Centric)	37%	34%	43%	30%	56%	40%	32%	50%	37%
Bottom 2 Box (Net) (Person-Centered)	12%	9%	20%	27%	4%	20%	9%	3%	21%

Q: Where your organization is today - FROM: Population-Centric (7) Uses, TO: Person-Centered (1) (N=241)

Source: 2017 Prophet Healthcare Consumerism Study
Respondents are healthcare executives across the globe

Reported Progress on Shift 4

BOLD	HIGH
UNDERLINED	MEDIUM
ITALIZED	LOW

	TOTAL	U.S.	U.K.	Germany	China	Japan	Provider	Payer	Pharma
	X	A	B	C	D	E	F	G	H
BASE	241.0	146.0	30*	30*	25**	10**	105.0	40*	96*
Top 2 Box (Net) (Incremental Improvements)	35%	34%	33%	*27%*	52%	40%	32%	55%	30%
Bottom 2 Box (Net) (Pervasive Innovation)	12%	9%	20%	13%	12%	30%	13%	–	15%

Q: Where your organization is today - FROM: Incremental Improvements (7), TO: Pervasive Innovation (1) (N=241)

Source: 2017 Prophet Healthcare Consumerism Study
Respondents are healthcare executives across the globe

Reported Progress on Shift 5

BOLD	HIGH
UNDERLINED	MEDIUM
ITALIZED	LOW

	TOTAL	U.S.	U.K.	Germany	China	Japan	Provider	Payer	Pharma
	X	A	B	C	D	E	F	G	H
BASE	241.0	146.0	30*	30*	25**	10**	105.0	40*	96*
Top 2 Box (Net) (Insights as a Function)	32%	*25%*	53%	*23%*	60%	30%	29%	48%	30%
Bottom 2 Box (Net) (Culture of Consumer Obsession)	15%	14%	10%	23%	16%	20%	14%	15%	16%

Q: Where your organization is today - FROM: Insights as function (7), TO: Culture of Consumer Obsession (1) (N=241)

Source: 2017 Prophet Healthcare Consumerism Study
Respondents are healthcare executives across the globe

PROPHET'S BRAND RELEVANCE INDEX

At Prophet, we believe the strongest brands are the ones that are relentlessly relevant and making a difference in consumers' lives. We created the Prophet Brand Relevance Index™ (BRI) to understand the principles that great brands execute against — in customers' minds — in order to establish themselves as relentlessly relevant and to help companies measure brand relevance and understand how it can unlock growth.

Relevant brands make bold moves that amaze customers, push competitors out of consideration, and – at times – define entirely new categories and markets. And they do it while remaining unwaveringly authentic to who they are. Those companies that have built relentlessly relevant brands generally have four common characteristics:

Characteristics of a Relentlessly Relevant Brand

Customer Obsessed	*Brands we can't imagine living without Everything these brands invest in, create and bring to market is designed to meet important needs in people's lives.*
Ruthlessly Pragmatic	*Brands we depend on These brands make sure their products are available where and when customers need them, deliver consistent experiences, and simply make life easier for their customers.*
Distinctively Inspired	*Brands that inspire us These brands make emotional connections, earn trust and often exist to fulfill a larger purpose.*
Pervasively Innovative	*Brands that consistently innovate These brands don't rest on their laurels. Even as industry leaders they push the status quo, engage with customers in new and creative ways, and find new ways to address unmet needs.*

In 2017, Prophet surveyed 50,000 consumers in China, Germany, United Kingdom and United States to determine which 750 unique brands they simply cannot live without. Companies from all industries that contribute materially to household spend in each respective market were included in the study. The data was sourced from the Bureau of Labor Statistics' February 2016 Report on Consumer Expenditures (US), Office for National Statistics' 2015 Report (Germany), and McKinsey's Macroeconomic China Model Update for 2015 (China). Within each industry, the companies that were included achieved outsized business performance (MRY revenues and trailing 3-year revenue growth) within their respective industries. In some instances, smaller companies that have been driving change in these industries were also included given their significant traction with consumers. 750 unique brands, including 150 global brands and 600 regional brands, were rated across the four regional studies. Brands not included were those in the tobacco and firearms categories and companies engaged solely or primarily in business-to-business (B2B) categories. Below are the top ten brands from each region:

Prophet Brand Relevence Index: Top Brands

TOP 10 Brands in U.S.

01	02	03	04	05	06	07	08	09	10
Apple	Google	amazon	NETFLIX	Pinterest	android	Spotify	PIXAR	Disney	SAMSUNG

TOP 10 Brands in U.K.

01	02	03	04	05	06	07	08	09	10
Apple	Google	android	LEGO	Spotify	NETFLIX	dyson	LUSH	PlayStation	amazon

TOP 10 Brands in Germany

01	02	03	04	05	06	07	08	09	10
Apple	amazon	Google	android	LEGO	Spotify	PlayStation	Miele	PayPal	WhatsApp

TOP 10 Brands in China

01	02	03	04	05	06	07	08	09	10
支付宝 ALIPAY	WeChat	android	IKEA	Apple	Nike		BMW	Marriott	

PROPHET / GE HEALTHCARE PARTNERS STUDY OF PATIENT EXPERIENCE

As we have discovered in *Making the Healthcare Shift* there is a vital change happening in healthcare: people are demanding to be treated as savvy consumers, who deserve choices, convenience and fair prices. The same revolution of consumerism that's shaking up the way the world buys financial services, airline tickets and groceries is finally underway in healthcare. And as healthcare options multiply, this trend will only accelerate. Providers who are ready to respond by creating a strong patient experience are going to win, and those who aren't will be left behind.

To better understand the consumer healthcare experience, Prophet partnered with GE Healthcare Partners to assess the gap between patient and providers' expectations and perceptions.

Prophet routinely sees healthcare patients frustrated with the current system and providers struggling to meet the needs of savvy consumers. GE Healthcare Partners often works with providers struggling to balance their competing priorities of cost efficiency, care delivery transformation, and patient experience. Together we wanted to better understand and quantify this divide and to help providers better address healthcare consumers' most pressing needs.

A 2015 survey was conducted online, with consumers and providers. Of the 3,000 respondents, consumers were between the ages of 18 and 65 and were a representative sample of the general population, and indicated that they are a healthcare decision maker or influencer in their household. The 300 responding providers needed to be a senior executive (Vice President or higher) at institutions that employed at least 20 physicians. Respondents were not compensated for their participation.

Here are some of our findings:

Despite the best intentions to deliver a better patient experience, providers struggle to make it a priority among competing initiatives

Gaps Between Provider Intentions and Patient Experience

	PROVIDERS SAY...	PROVIDERS DO...
Priorities	75% *believe PX is important to their future success*	*On the list of hospital CEO's top concerns, patient satisfaction is* **not in the top five***
Experience Strategy	90% *claim to have a patient experience strategy*	24% *believe they are delivering extremely well on the strategy*
Investments	91% *believe digital transformation is important*	29% *are investing in digital tools and online presence*
Customer Understanding	70% *claim to have a holistic view of their patient base*	15% *really understand patient needs*
Technology	42% *believe technologies related to patient outreach and engagement are extremely important in driving experiences*	26% *actually deliver these patient outreach and engagement technologies today*

Source: 2016 Prophet/GE Healthcare Partners Patient Experience Study

Providers misjudge the perception of their performance on elements that are most important to consumers

Gaps in Perceptions of Provider Performance

% Who Believe Providers Delivering Good / Excellent Patient Experience

PROVIDERS
63%

23%
Gap

CONSUMERS
40%

% Agreeing (Top 3 Box %)

PROVIDERS   CONSUMERS

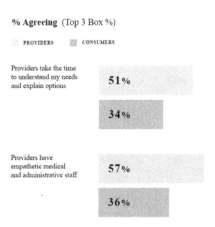

Providers take the time to understand my needs and explain options
51%
34%

Providers have empathetic medical and administrative staff
57%
36%

Q1. How well do you feel providers are delivering on the entire PX? (N=3,000), Top 3 Box % shown, 7 point scale

Q2. How well do you feel your organization is delivering on the entire PX? (N=300), Top 3 Box % shown, 7 point scale

Source: 2016 Prophet/GE Healthcare Partners Patient Experience Study

A17. How well do you feel hospitals are delivering on each of these? (N=3000)

A24. How well do you think your org. is performing on the aspects of the PX? (N=300)

Source: 2016 Prophet/GE Healthcare Partners Patient Experience Study

Gaps between provider and patient perceptions exist for multiple aspects, some greater than others

Consumer vs. Provider Performance
(Top 3 Box %, 7 point scale)

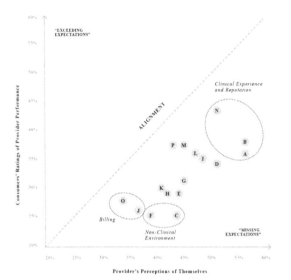

A.	Has empathetic medical and administrative staff
B.	Has a great reputation
C.	Provides healthy and enticing food options within their facility
D.	Takes the time to understand my needs and explain options
E.	Has quality and comfortable decor and furniture
F.	Provides services to make visit more convenient and comfortable
G.	Offers ways for me to review my health records online
H.	Coordinates care for me with people outside the facility
I.	Communicates results of diagnostic tests in a timely manner
J.	Has a transparent billing process
K.	Allows me to see the doctor I want, when I want
L.	Makes scheduling appointments quick and easy
M.	Provides clear direction and support for care post-visit
N.	Uses state of the art devices
O.	Has a simple billing process
P.	Uses state of the art software systems

Provider's Perceptions of Themselves

Providers continue to have a limited view of where the patient experience applies

How Providers Define the Patient Experience

19%

The experiences and interactions from a patient's single visit

19%

Any experiences the patient has within our facility over multiple visits

33%

All experiences the patient has with our system of care over multiple visits

31%

All things related to a patients health

CUMULATIVE

| 19% | 36% | 69% | 100% |

Q: How does your organization define patient experience? (N=252)

Source: 2016 Prophet/GE Healthcare Partners Patient Experience Study

Morgan James
Speakers Group

www.TheMorganJamesSpeakersGroup.com

We connect Morgan James published
authors with live and online events
and audiences who will benefit
from their expertise.

CPSIA information can be obtained
at www.ICGtesting.com
Printed in the USA
BVHW071926021118
531613BV00002B/2/P